UNBREAKABLE
DAILY BIBLE PLAN

MANTOUR MINISTRIES

Design: James J. Holden

Subject Headings:
1. Christian life 2. Men's Ministry 3. Spiritual Growth

ISBN 978-1-7378821-9-0

Printed in the United States of America

WEEK ONE

THE CHARACTERISTIC OF THE GOOD OR THE GREAT MAN IS NOT THAT HE HAS BEEN EXEMPT FROM THE EVILS OF LIFE, BUT THAT HE HAS SURMOUNTED THEM.[1]
-PATRICK HENRY

These words spoken by Patrick Henry describe what God has placed on my heart to share with men today. It's time for God's men to become unbreakable men.

It has broken my heart over the past few years to see so many men of God be broken and lying on the mat, with the enemy standing in triumph over them.

Pastors leave their churches after falling into sin.

Husbands lose their marriages because they are defeated by temptation.

Finances were in ruin because men were broken under the burden of debt.

Reputations are destroyed because of lives lived in secret and deceit.

The list goes on and on.

The world is filled with too many broken, defeated men. It is time to get off the mat and get back in the fight.

It is not God's will for His men to live broken, defeated lives. He ordained for His children to be victorious.

God is calling His men to get back into the fight.   No man has to stay broken and defeated. There is hope!

Guys, it is time to get up off the mat and get back into the fight! You cannot stay living broken and defeated! Victory is there for you. Through God, you are unbreakable!

You can conquer. You can end the fight with your arms raised high in victory as your enemies lay knocked out at your feet.

You can become unbreakable!

This Bible Plan has two purposes.

First, it's to help you get into God's Word. We cannot survive in today's world amidst all the lies and deceit if we do not know and recognize the truth of the Bible. The Bible is our weapon to fight back against the lies. Our hope for you is that each day, you take a few minutes to read the suggested Bible passages, immersing yourself in the Word of God.

Second, we want these weekly devotionals to be a shot in the arm to help you as you live each day for God. This year, we are looking at great quotes and what we can learn from them. Some are from the *Rocky* franchise and other movies, some are words of historical men, and some are taken directly from God's Word. Each is designed to help you grow spiritually and to become an unbreakable, victorious man of God.

Are you ready to join me over the next 52 weeks to become an unbreakable man dedicated to God and His Word?

Will you allow the Bible to speak to you, bringing hope, motivation, conviction, and strength as you realize God's mercy, compassion, grace, and holiness found in His Word?

I'm thrilled to stand arm-in-arm with you as we learn to be unbreakable men together.

SUNDAY
☐ Genesis 1-2

☐ Revelation 1:1-9

MONDAY
☐ Genesis 3

☐ Revelation 1:9-20

TUESDAY
☐ Genesis 4-5

☐ Revelation 2

WEDNESDAY
☐ Genesis 6-7

☐ Revelation 3

THURSDAY
☐ Genesis 8-9

☐ Revelation 4

FRIDAY
☐ Genesis 10

☐ Revelation 5

NOTES AND REFLECTION

MEMORY VERSE

For you have need of endurance, so that when you have done the will of God you may receive what is promised. -Hebrews 10:36

WEEK TWO

THREE YEARS AGO YOU WAS SUPERNATURAL. YOU WAS HARD AND YOU WAS NASTY AND YOU HAD THIS CAST-IRON JAW, BUT THEN THE WORST THING HAPPENED TO YOU, THAT COULD HAPPEN TO ANY FIGHTER. YOU GOT CIVILIZED.
-MICK

In *Rocky III* (my favorite of the Rocky movies), Rocky Balboa, now the World Champion, has gone from struggling to living a life of wealth and luxury after winning his rematch against Apollo Creed. The movie shows Rocky easily defending his title against inferior opponents, enjoying fame and fortune. Meanwhile, Clubber Lang, played by Mr. T, trains hard and harbors resentment towards Rocky's success.

At a ceremony dedicating a statue of Rocky in Philadelphia, Rocky announces his retirement. This angers Clubber Lang, leading to a heated confrontation where Rocky agrees to one last fight against him. Rocky's manager, Mick, is furious, knowing Rocky has fought easy opponents and is no longer the fighter he once was. Mick tells Rocky he can't win against Clubber.

In this scene, we hear Mick's words, *"You got civilized."*[1]

Sadly, I believe these words ring true for too many of God's sons. Too many of God's men are like Rocky. They started their walk with God with passion and fire. They wanted Him more than they wanted their next breath. They spent time with Him, learning what He was like and how they could become like Him. Then, the worst thing happened to them that can happen to a Christian…they got civilized. They got complacent. Christianity became going to church and doing things for God, and they lost their passion for being with God.

Rocky became complacent, losing his hunger and passion for boxing. In the end, Clubber Lang defeated him.

Too many of God's men are in the same place spiritually. We haven't walked away from God. We haven't abandoned our faith. But we don't have the same passion and hunger we used to have. We lost our passion.

I am not trying to discourage or condemn anyone. However, just like with Rocky, losing our spiritual passion is a dangerous place to be.

Why do I say that? Let's look at Revelation 3:2-5 to see what God says about complacent Christians.

> *I know all the things you do. I have seen your hard work and your patient endurance. I know you don't tolerate evil people. You have examined the claims of those who say they are apostles but are not. You have discovered they are liars. You have patiently suffered for me without quitting.*
>
> *But I have this complaint against you. You don't love me or each other as you did at first!*
>
> *Look how far you have fallen! Turn back to me and do the works you did at first. If you don't repent, I will come and remove your lampstand from its place among the churches. (NLT)*

The church in Ephesus had become civilized. It forgot its first love. It lost the joy it had when it first got saved and began following God.

The years of ministry and serving God, mixed with persecution and church issues, left them serving out of a sense of duty, not love and relationship with God. The passion, the fire, and the joy they had when they first came to God were gone.

Notice God says, *"Look how far you have fallen."* He didn't view this lack of passion as a good thing or spiritual maturity. He hated it. He hated the loss of fellowship and the closeness that He no longer experienced with the Ephesian church. He longed for them to see they had become weary in well-doing and lost their fire and zeal. It was church activity and business, not service out of love and gratitude. He wanted to change them. He wanted them to long for Him.

Does this ring true in your life? If so, how do you fix it? How do you get back to our First Love? Thankfully, the passage in Revelations gives us the answers.

1. Consider how far you have fallen

Take a moment to remember what your life was like when you first became a Christian. How did you feel? What did you do? How much time did you spend in prayer? Did you have a passion for reading the Bible? Do you remember the excitement you felt? Do you recall the trust you had in God? Remember how praise welled up inside of you? Stop and think about the weeks and months after you first came to Christ and see if you still feel the same way. Has your love and passion dwindled? Reflecting on this is the first step to returning to your first love.

2. Repent

The passage clearly states that we must repent for losing our first love. We must ask God for forgiveness for becoming so busy doing things for Him that we lose sight of the wonderful opportunity to be with Him. We should ask Him to forgive us for not being as dedicated, passionate, and eager for Him. We need to seek His forgiveness and ask for restoration.

3. Do the things you did at first

The last thing we need to do is return to the way things used to be. We must wholeheartedly pursue God in our lives. We need to restore our passion and ask God to bring back the joy we once had.

God desires for His children to return to the love they had when they first came to Him. He wants our relationship to be as passionate and exciting as it was initially. He waits for us to realize that we have drifted away. He is waiting for us to repent for allowing our hearts to grow cold, and He is waiting with open arms for us to be restored. He wants us to have a close relationship with Him. Will you return to the passionate man you used to be, or will you remain a civilized, unfulfilled believer?

SUNDAY
- [ ] Psalms 1-3

MONDAY
- [ ] Genesis 11-12
- [ ] Revelation 6

TUESDAY
- [ ] Genesis 13-14
- [ ] Revelation 7

WEDNESDAY
- [ ] Genesis 15-16
- [ ] Revelation 8

THURSDAY
- [ ] Genesis 17-18
- [ ] Revelation 9

FRIDAY
- [ ] Genesis 19-20
- [ ] Revelation 10

NOTES AND REFLECTION

MEMORY VERSE

I appeal to you therefore, brothers, by the mercies of God, to present your bodies as a living sacrifice, holy and acceptable to God, which is your spiritual worship. Do not be conformed to this world, but be transformed by the renewal of your mind, that by testing you may discern what is the will of God, what is good and acceptable and perfect. -Romans 12:1-2

WEEK THREE

WE HELD THE GREATEST TITLE IN THE WHOLE WORLD, BABE. YOU LOST THAT FIGHT FOR ALL THE WRONG REASONS. YOU LOST YOUR EDGE. ALL RIGHT, I KNOW YOUR MANAGER DYING HAD YOU ALL MESSED UP INSIDE, BUT THE TRUTH IS YOU DIDN'T LOOK HUNGRY. NOW WHEN WE FOUGHT, YOU HAD THAT EYE OF THE TIGER, MAN, THE EDGE. AND NOW YOU GOTTA GET IT BACK, AND THE WAY TO GET IT BACK IS TO GO BACK TO THE BEGINNING. YOU KNOW WHAT I MEAN? EYE OF THE TIGER, MAN.[1] -APOLLO CREED

Last week, we discussed how Rocky had lost his edge; he got civilized, as Mick said. This week, I want to look at the second part of *Rocky III* and one of the greatest lines uttered in a movie.

"Eye of the Tiger." [1]

Rocky didn't listen to Mick's advice, fought Clubber Lang, and was defeated. But he didn't stay down, thanks to his old opponent-now-turned-friend, Apollo Creed.

Apollo knew what Mick had tried to tell Rocky was true. He knew Rocky had become complacent, and he had to get back to the mindset of a fighter. He had to regain the Eye of the Tiger!

I am tired of seeing my brothers in Christ lying flat on the mat, defeated and knocked down. God didn't create us to live a defeated life. He promised us victory! We need to get on our feet and fight once again!

Apollo took Rocky back to his old gym to be around young, hungry boxers. He showed Rocky the passion in them to win, to be great, and to become the best. Apollo said, *"See that look in their eyes, Rock? You gotta get that look back, Rock. Eye of the Tiger, man."*[1]

Eye of the Tiger! Men, we need to get that look back! EYE OF THE TIGER! We need the old passion back! We must remember where we came from and how God set us free. We have to remember the mess we were. We need to recall the wretched future that awaited us before God set us free. Eye of the Tiger!

We need to remember the gratitude and love we felt for God initially. We need to reclaim the same passion for God we had in the beginning! Eye of the Tiger, men, Eye of the Tiger!

We must regain the fervor for the things of God we once had. We have to reclaim our desire to spend time with Him. Like Rocky, we have to get back into training. We have to work hard. We have to sweat and labor to reclaim our fire for God. **EYE OF THE TIGER!**

We can do it! Like Rocky, we can regain our fire. Men live defeated because they lost their passion for God and for loving and pleasing Him. But we can get it back! We can overcome complacency. We can rebuild our relationship. We can be victorious! How do we do it?

The old-fashioned way! Through hard work, perseverance, and sacrifice. Rocky had to develop a new training regimen, try different approaches and methods, learn to fight differently, and endure blood, sweat, and tears to regain his crown. But in the end, HE was the one with the Eye of the Tiger, and he was the one who stood victorious!

We can be victorious again! Sin doesn't need to control us. Bondage doesn't need to defeat us. Addiction doesn't need to define us. We can have victory!

Recapture your *"eye of the tiger,"* your zeal.

We have to go at it with 110% of our being. We need radical change. We must pursue God and His ways with a passion and fervor that surpasses what we had when we were first saved. We need to give it all we have. Eye of the Tiger!

We need to get back to where we used to be. Apollo told Rocky he had to get that look back. We must return to pursuing God in our lives wholeheartedly. We need the passion restored. We should ask God to restore the joy we once had.

King David prayed an excellent prayer we can all pray. David was a man after God's heart. He wanted to love and serve God more than anything in the world. However, over time, he lost sight of spending time with God as he served God as king of Israel. He lost the Eye of the Tiger and stayed behind while his men went to war. As a result, David fell to temptation, had an affair with a married woman, and murdered her husband to keep his sins under wraps.

David wasn't able to keep it quiet. The prophet Nathan confronted David and pointed out David's sin. David immediately repented of his sins. Thankfully, we have this repentant prayer recorded in Psalm 51. After David repents of his sin, he remembers the relationship he used to have, and he asks God to forgive him. Let's read part of His prayer.

> ***Create in me a pure heart, O God, and renew a steadfast spirit within me. Do not cast me from Your presence or take Your Holy Spirit from me. Restore to me the joy of Your salvation and grant me a willing spirit, to sustain me. -Psalm 51:10-12 (NIV)***

Notice this prayer is a petition to God to restore the joy of his salvation. He wanted God to restore him to where he had fallen. This is an excellent example for all of us to follow.

God desires for His children to return to the passion and hunger they had when they first came to Him. He wants our relationship with Him to be as passionate and exciting as it was when we first sought Him. He waits for us to realize that we have strayed from this passion and to repent for allowing our hearts to grow cold. With open arms, He waits for us to be restored to where we once were, desiring a close and meaningful relationship with us.

Are there areas in your life where your love for God has become a sense of duty?

Do you still feel the same joy and passion you had when you first believed in Christ?

Have complacency and spiritual exhaustion from constantly doing good works hindered your relationship with God?

These are essential questions.

We must reflect on our lives and see if we have lost the fervor we once had for God. Then, we must return to the place from where we drifted. We must do this today!

Reclaim that Eye of the Tiger!

SUNDAY
- [ ] Psalms 4-6

MONDAY
- [ ] Genesis 21-22
- [ ] Revelation 11

TUESDAY
- [ ] Genesis 23-24
- [ ] Revelation 12

WEDNESDAY
- [ ] Genesis 25-26
- [ ] Revelation 13

THURSDAY
- [ ] Genesis 27-28
- [ ] Revelation 14

FRIDAY
- [ ] Genesis 29-30
- [ ] Revelation 15

NOTES AND REFLECTION

MEMORY VERSE

Therefore, since we are surrounded by so great a cloud of witnesses, let us also lay aside every weight, and sin which clings so closely, and let us run with endurance the race that is set before us. -Hebrews 12:1

Week Four

BE ON GUARD; STAND FIRM IN THE FAITH; BE COURAGEOUS; BE STRONG. -PAUL THE APOSTLE, 1 COR. 16:13, (NLT)

I love Paul. He says the hard stuff out loud and doesn't pull his punches. These words in 1 Corinthians 16:13 are as true today as they were when he initially said them.

Our world is trying to knock men out. They want to feminize us, demonize us, and bring us under the modernistic view of manhood. I work every day encouraging men to block the world's roundhouses that are trying to lay them out on the mat.

The world needs men who follow Paul's words. This quote contains four commands. Let's examine each individually.

1. Be on your guard.

Yesterday, I was watching *Rocky II*. In one scene, Rocky tells Mick he wants to fight again. Mick tells him that while Rocky has heart, he physically can't do it. His depth of vision was shot from the beating he took in his first fight with Apollo Creed. Mick basically says he wouldn't be able to see Apollo's punches coming at him. He wouldn't be able to guard against them, and he'd get knocked out or killed.

A fighter must always be alert and aware of the coming attacks. We cannot have a blind spot in our lives, or the enemy will exploit it and knock us out. Men, know your weaknesses, be aware of your struggles, know where you are vulnerable, and be ready to defend yourself at all times.

2. Stand Firm in the Faith

It is essential today to know what you believe and why you believe it and then stand firm for your beliefs. The world wants you to compromise. Progressive Christians are rewriting the Bible to fit their whims and desires. We must stand firm on the Word of God and refuse to bend. Every whim of society cannot sway us. Instead, we must know the truth of God's Word and live it daily.

The enemy wants to knock you down; you must stand firm as an unbreakable man!

3. Be courageous.

An unbreakable man is a courageous man. He doesn't back down; he doesn't surrender.

The ESV uses the phrase *"act like a man"* in its translation in place of the words *"be courageous."* I find this fascinating. It is as if they see being courageous as an indelible characteristic of a man.

Webster's dictionary defines courage as *"the mental or moral strength to venture, persevere, and withstand danger, fear, or difficulty."*[1]

Men of God need to withstand fears that stop them in their tracks. We do this through the power of God.

2 Timothy 1:7 says: **"For God has not given us a spirit of fear, but of power and of love and of a sound mind."** (NKJV)

Fear is the opposite of what we are called to do: be courageous men. When courage defines us, we stand as unbreakable men.

4. Be Strong

I despise the attempted feminization of manhood in our world. God created man and woman with distinct traits and characteristics.

Both have unique strengths that complement each other, and both sets of strengths are needed and necessary.

The world wants to label male characteristics as *"toxic."* **GOD DOESN'T MAKE TOXIC MEN!**

Yes, men sometimes make bad decisions that lead to sin. But they weren't created to be toxic. No man is created to be an abuser, a liar, or a deceiver. No man is created to degrade women and put them down or abuse them. God didn't design anyone to ever hurt a child. In their sin, men make decisions to act toxically, but they weren't created toxic.

God makes leaders—men who understand Biblical servant leadership. He made us the strong pillar, the support, and the foundation of stability for those in our lives.

It isn't toxic to be an unbreakable man! It is our calling.

The enduring words of Paul the Apostle resonate today as much as they did in the past. His call to vigilance, unwavering faith, courage, and strength remains powerful in a world that often seeks to undermine traditional masculinity. Men must remain vigilant, stand firm in their beliefs, embody courage in the face of challenges, and exemplify unyielding strength. It's how God designed us to be. When we embrace these four principles, men can become unshakeable pillars of stability and support, embracing their calling with unwavering commitment and resolve. Such a man is an unbreakable man!

SUNDAY
- [ ] Psalms 7-10

MONDAY
- [ ] Genesis 31-32
- [ ] Revelation 16

TUESDAY
- [ ] Genesis 33-34
- [ ] Revelation 17

WEDNESDAY
- [ ] Genesis 35-36
- [ ] Revelation 18

THURSDAY
- [ ] Genesis 37-38
- [ ] Revelation 19

FRIDAY
- [ ] Genesis 39-40
- [ ] Revelation 20

NOTES AND REFLECTION

MEMORY VERSE

Looking to Jesus, the founder and perfecter of our faith, who for the joy that was set before him endured the cross, despising the shame, and is seated at the right hand of the throne of God.
-Hebrews 12:2

WEEK FIVE

Associate with men of good quality if you esteem your own reputation; it is far better to be alone, than to be in bad company.[1] -George Washington

George Washington, the first President of the United States, spoke these words. This timeless wisdom reinforces the time-honored Biblical principle that the company we keep significantly influences our character and our walk with God.

The Bible is jam-packed with words encouraging us to choose our companions wisely.

Proverbs 13:20 says: *"Become wise by walking with the wise; hang out with fools and watch your life fall to pieces." (MSG)*

This verse reminds us that our relationships shape us for better or worse. Walking with the wise leads to wisdom, but associating with fools leads to harm.

In today's world, where the pressure to conform is intense, it's crucial for Christian men to stand firm in their faith and make deliberate choices about their associations. Surrounding ourselves with godly men not only encourages us to live righteously, grow spiritually, and maintain our integrity, but also provides a strong support system. On the flip side, when we surround ourselves with those who do not share our values, we open ourselves up to be led into sin and tarnish our witness for Christ.

It's essential to think about who our friends are.

Are your closest friends drawing you closer to God or pulling you away from Him?

Are they encouraging you to live out your faith boldly, or are they tempting you to compromise your values?

Next, find godly influences to be around you. Proverbs 27:17 says, *"As iron sharpens iron, so a friend sharpens a friend."* *(NLT)*

Actively seek out the company of godly men who will challenge you, hold you accountable, and support you in your walk with Christ. Join a men's Bible study, prayer group, or fellowship where you can build meaningful, Christ-centered relationships.

Also, guys, remember friendship is a two-way street. Proverbs 18:24 says, *"Friends come, and friends go, but a true friend sticks by you like family."* *(MSG)*

Strive to be the kind of friend who inspires others to pursue righteousness. Your influence can be a powerful testimony of God's love and truth. Encourage your friends in their faith journeys, pray for them, and stand by them in times of trial.

Remember, as President Washington wisely said, the company you keep shapes your character and your destiny. Choose wisely, and let your friendships reflect your commitment to Christ. It is far better to walk alone with God than to be in bad company. Thankfully, you don't have to be alone when you surround yourself with other godly, unbreakable men.

SUNDAY
☐ Psalms 11-14

MONDAY
☐ Genesis 41-42

☐ Revelation 21

TUESDAY
☐ Genesis 43-44

☐ Revelation 22

WEDNESDAY
☐ Genesis 45-46

☐ Matthew 1

THURSDAY
☐ Genesis 47-48

☐ Matthew 2

FRIDAY
☐ Genesis 49-50

☐ Matthew 3

NOTES AND REFLECTION

MEMORY VERSE

Consider him who endured from sinners such hostility against himself, so that you may not grow weary or fainthearted. -Hebrews 12:3

WEEK SIX

HOW THEN COULD I DO SUCH A WICKED THING AND SIN AGAINST GOD? -JOSEPH

Have you ever heard of a rags-to-riches story? This is when a poor person finds success and fame. Hollywood has made billions off of such stories. The story of Joseph in the Bible wouldn't fall into this category. Instead, Joseph would be a from riches-to-rags-to-riches-to-rags-to-riches story.

Joseph grew up with a silver spoon in his mouth. He was the center of his father's universe and, honestly, a bit spoiled. However, amidst all this, beat the heart of a man who loved and served God.

After his jealous brothers changed their plans from killing him to selling him as a slave, Joseph found himself in a very different place. He was now a slave forced into servitude. But God had a plan for Joseph because He saw a tender heart inside him.

Joseph was an intelligent, talented man, but more importantly, he had the anointing of God on him. Because of this, he became the head slave of the second most powerful man in Egypt, Potiphar. The Bible says everything Joseph touched prospered, and Joseph was living pretty well, albeit as a slave.

Another fact about Joseph was that, in addition to being smart, capable, talented, spirit-led, and anointed, the dude was a stud—the Brad Pitt of Potiphar's house. This didn't go unnoticed by Potiphar's wife.

Mrs. Potiphar, not one for being subtle, made sexual pass after sexual pass. Each time, Joseph refused.

Can you imagine how hard this was for Joseph as he refused her daily advances? He was a young man. He was a virgin. He was far away from his family and friends. He was lonely. He felt rejected. His older brothers had just sold him. He had sexual desires. He could have very easily found comfort in the arms of this more-than-willing woman.

But instead, Joseph rejected her advances each time. How did he find the strength to do it? Because he loved Someone more than he loved his own sexual gratification. Look at his words.

> **How then can I do this great wickedness and sin against God? -Genesis 39:9 (ESV)**

Joseph refused to sin against his God.

Joseph knew something that Mrs. Potiphar didn't know...his life was an open book before God, and he could not commit such blatant sin against his God. He was an ordinary young man with the same desires we all face, but Joseph's God was more real to him than anything or anyone else on earth. Instead, He chose to walk away.

Men, we need to have the same attitude when it comes to sexual temptation. We need to see it as a sin against God.

Having sex with anyone who is not your married partner is a sin against God. I can't put it any more bluntly.

Whether it is pre-marital sex or an affair, it is a sin. It goes against God's perfect design of sex being only between a husband and wife. This is God's order for family life.

God disapproves of us having sex in the wrong place and at the wrong time. Sex in the wrong place is also known as pornography.

How is porn sex in the wrong place? Watching porn isn't really having sex, is it? Well, let's look at what Jesus says.

Matthew 5:27-28 says, ***"You have heard that it was said, 'You shall not commit adultery.' But I tell you that anyone who looks at a woman with lustful intent has already committed adultery with her in his heart." (ESV)***

In God's eyes, porn is the same as having sex; it says so right there. Sex is meant for the marriage bed, not a dark room in front of a computer screen. The wrong place is alone in a room with a computer screen.

Many men see this as an impossible standard. They feel they have a right to look at a pretty girl and fantasize about her. However, Jesus makes it clear. You don't. If we look at a woman lustfully, if we fantasize about a woman, it is a sin against God. There is no way around it.

Sex in the wrong time is sex with anyone who isn't your wife, whether you are single or married.

Sex was created to be between a husband and a wife. Having an affair in marriage will damage your relationships. It causes life-changing damage to the spouse and children involved. It hurts co-workers, friends, and churches. It is not just a private act. It kills many relationships and destroys reputations.

If you're single, having sex before marriage will damage your future marriage relationship. God does not condone sex before marriage. He understands all the baggage this will cause to your future relationship, so we single guys need to abstain from sex and save it for our wedding night.

To have pre-marital sex or an affair is to be anti-family and anti-God. An affair is cheating on the wife you took a sacred vow with on your wedding day. Single guys, sex before marriage is not God's design for sex. Sex is for marriage. Period. As men, we have a responsibility to stay sexually pure.

The good news is that we have examples in life that show us that sexual purity can be done. Like Joseph, we can refuse to sin against God and give in to sexual sin.

An unbreakable man refuses to sin sexually against God. He realizes it will cause separation between him and God, so he stands firm and stays pure like Joseph.

SUNDAY
☐ Psalms 15-17

MONDAY
☐ Proverbs 1-2

☐ Matthew 4

TUESDAY
☐ Proverbs 3-4

☐ Matthew 5

WEDNESDAY
☐ Proverbs 5-6

☐ Matthew 6

THURSDAY
☐ Proverbs 7-8

☐ Matthew 7

FRIDAY
☐ Proverbs 9-10

☐ Matthew 8

NOTES AND REFLECTION

MEMORY VERSE

In your struggle against sin you have not yet resisted to the point of shedding your blood.
-Hebrews 12:4

WEEK SEVEN

EVERYBODY CAN BE GREAT...BECAUSE ANYBODY CAN SERVE. YOU DON'T HAVE TO HAVE A COLLEGE DEGREE TO SERVE. YOU DON'T HAVE TO MAKE YOUR SUBJECT AND VERB AGREE TO SERVE. YOU ONLY NEED A HEART FULL OF GRACE. A SOUL GENERATED BY LOVE.[1] -MARTIN LUTHER KING, JR.

Recently, I had the pleasure of spending the day with two of my favorite people in the world, a beautiful six-year-old and her adorable 4-year-old brother and their parents. I love getting to spend time with these kids and playing with them. They bring me such joy. Whether it be a rousing game of monkey in the middle, or telling each other knock-knock jokes and tooting jokes (they call passing gas *"tooting"*), we always have a blast. They are my best buddies!

At one point, we were playing outside on the deck. The parents didn't want the kids in the house at this point. They wanted them outside to burn off some energy. However, the little guy kept trying to go inside the house. I told him, *"You're supposed to play out here with me. Don't go in the house. "*

A few minutes later, Adessa got up and walked off to the house, and the little boy ran after her like a shot. I didn't think anything of it because he was with Adessa. A few minutes later, he came running up to me with a big smile on his face and proudly proclaimed to me, *"Hey Jamie, you're not the boss. Adessa's the boss. "*

Well, his older sister heard what he said and thought it was so funny, so for the next hour, I had two little voices repeating over and over, *"Jamie's not the boss; Adessa's the boss. "*

Apparently, this little guy had run up to Adessa to tell her she wasn't allowed in the house either. Adessa asked why she couldn't go in, and he replied, *"Jamie said we're not allowed in the house."* Adessa replied, *"Well, Jamie is not my boss."* Thus, the chorus of *"Jamie's not the boss, Adessa's the boss"* began.

It was so funny, but unfortunately, too often, people think being *"the boss"* means they get to be in charge, telling others what to do, and they have to listen. Matthew 20:26-28 tells us the opposite when Jesus says, ***"Not so with you. Instead, whoever wants to become great among you must be your servant, and whoever wants to be first must be your slave— just as the Son of Man did not come to be served, but to serve, and to give his life as a ransom for many."*** *(NIV)*

The backdrop for this Scripture is interesting. Jesus had just finished teaching His disciples, including telling them about His death (which they did not want to hear), when the mother of James and John asked Him a favor. And it was a doozy!

Believe it or not, she asked if her sons could sit at Jesus' right and left hand when they came into His kingdom. Of course, the other disciples heard about this request and were ticked off. Jesus knew that, once again, His disciples needed another lesson on what it meant to be a leader in God's kingdom.

The disciples struggled with this teaching because they thought, as Jesus's right-hand men, they deserved to have the least of these serving them. This childish attitude came from a lifetime of the Jewish elite pushing them down and lording over them. Now they were the big wigs, Jesus chosen men, and they were all up for being the top dog others served.

However, Jesus never let them get away with it. Instead, He taught them what serving means and how to develop a servant's heart. He daily demonstrated this fact to them in how He interacted with them and the people. He even demonstrated servanthood when He washed their feet.

Over and over again, Jesus tried to teach them this lesson: In God's kingdom, leadership means being the first in line to serve.

The same lesson applies today: Our job as men of God is to serve.

How do we do that?

The answer is quite simple.

We follow Jesus's example because Jesus's life was the model of a man Who served.

> *Don't be selfish; don't try to impress others. Be humble, thinking of others as better than yourselves. Don't look out only for your own interests, but take an interest in others, too.*
>
> *You must have the same attitude that Christ Jesus had.*
>
> *Though he was God, he did not think of equality with God as something to cling to.*
>
> *Instead, he gave up his divine privileges; he took the humble position of a slave and was born as a human being.*
>
> *When he appeared in human form, he humbled himself in obedience to God and died a criminal's death on a cross.*
> *-Philippians 2:3-8 (NLT)*

Jesus left the glory of heaven and came to earth to serve others. He put other people's needs above His needs. Jesus constantly had thousands of people coming to Him and needing His help and assistance. They had urgent needs and needed His miraculous power to help them. Jesus never turned them away. Even when He was tired or hungry, He put their needs and issues above His needs.

Jesus even put the disciple's needs above His own.

Of course, Jesus' greatest act of servanthood was when He laid down His life on the cross.

As leaders, men are called to follow Jesus' example and exhibit servant leadership.

Whether it be serving our wives, children, communities, or churches, the question should never be, *"How can others serve me?"* but rather, *"What can I do to serve you?"*

Martin Luther King sums this attitude up perfectly:

"Everybody can be great…because anybody can serve. You don't have to have a college degree to serve. You don't have to make your subject and verb agree to serve. You only need a heart full of grace. A soul generated by love."[1]

Do you want to be an unbreakable leader in your family, community, job, or church?

Find a way to serve.

Study how Jesus served others and follow His example.

Don't ask what others can do for you, but ask how you can serve them.

Unbreakable servanthood—it's what Jesus lived and Who He called us to be.

SUNDAY
- [ ] Psalms 18-20

MONDAY
- [ ] Proverbs 11
- [ ] Matthew 9-10

TUESDAY
- [ ] Proverbs 12
- [ ] Matthew 11-12

WEDNESDAY
- [ ] Proverbs 13
- [ ] Matthew 13-14

THURSDAY
- [ ] Proverbs 14
- [ ] Matthew 15-16

FRIDAY
- [ ] Proverbs 15
- [ ] Matthew 17-18

NOTES AND REFLECTION

MEMORY VERSE

Therefore lift your drooping hands and strengthen your weak knees, and make straight paths for your feet, so that what is lame may not be put out of joint but rather be healed.
-Hebrews 12:12-13

WEEK EIGHT

WE CAN'T TURN BACK THE CLOCK. WE CAN'T HIDE ALL YOUR FLAWS, BUT WE CAN MAKE THEM YOUR STRENGTHS.[1] -TONY "LITTLE DUKE" EVERS, CREED III

In 2023, the world was blessed with another installment of the *Creed* franchise. Unfortunately, this version of *Creed* didn't include Rocky at all, which made it kind of hard for me to get behind the first time I watched it. It didn't feel like a *Rocky* movie. But I have to admit, it was still a really good movie!

In *Creed III*, we find an older Adonis Creed retiring and living his life as a promoter. He's married, raising his daughter, whom he adores, and living a good life in his L.A. mansion. Then, a friend from his past returns from jail, bringing with him many painful memories from his days suffering abuse in a foster care group home.

Dame, Adonis's childhood friend, was just released from jail. Throughout the movie, he manipulates Donnie, using Donnie's past mistakes and regrets against him. Eventually, he gets Donnie to put him in a title fight, and he wins the title.

Dame immediately changes his attitude toward Donnie. He threatens him by saying he will take everything Donnie has. Donnie is stuck in his past and ends up coming out of retirement to fight Dame.

This is when we get this quote. Donnie's trainer assesses Donnie's ability to fight, and he says, *"We can't turn back the clock. We can't hide all your flaws, but we can make them your strengths."*[1]

They begin to train him, and of course, he wins.

But this quote really stuck out to me. An unbreakable man understands this concept.

We often dwell on our mistakes, sins, or flaws in life. We might wish we could turn back the clock, erase our shortcomings, and present ourselves as perfect. But the truth is, we can't undo the past or hide what brings us shame.

The good news is that our weaknesses don't define us. What defines us is how we respond to them. The quote above reminds us that while we can't change the past or make ourselves perfect, we can transform our weaknesses into strengths through the power of God.

This idea echoes the message of the Apostle Paul in 2 Corinthians 12:9.

> *But he said to me, "My grace is sufficient for you, for my power is made perfect in weakness." Therefore I will boast all the more gladly about my weaknesses, so that Christ's power may rest on me. (NIV)*

Paul understood that his weaknesses were not something to be hidden or ashamed of but something through which God's power could be displayed.

God doesn't expect us to be perfect; He expects us to be authentic and open to His transforming power. Our weaknesses are opportunities for God to work in and through us. When we acknowledge our weaknesses, we invite God's strength to fill those gaps. This helps make us unbreakable men who win!

SUNDAY
- [ ] Psalms 21-23

MONDAY
- [ ] Proverbs 16-17
- [ ] Matthew 19-20

TUESDAY
- [ ] Proverbs 18-19
- [ ] Matthew 21

WEDNESDAY
- [ ] Proverbs 20-21
- [ ] Matthew 22

THURSDAY
- [ ] Proverbs 22-23
- [ ] Matthew 23

FRIDAY
- [ ] Proverbs 24-25
- [ ] Matthew 24

NOTES AND REFLECTION

MEMORY VERSE

Strive for peace with everyone, and for the holiness without which no one will see the Lord. -Hebrews 12:14

Week Nine

I MUST BREAK YOU.[1] -IVAN DRAGO

It is a classic quote from what many believe to be the best of all the *Rocky* movies (I'm not one of them, but this is a debate for another day). Rocky is in the center ring, in the heart of Russia, touching his gloves before the fight with the Russian giant. Towering over Rocky, Drago, the *Siberian Bull*, pounds his gloves against Rocky's gloves, stares him in the eyes, and coldly, emotionlessly says those four intimidating words.

"I Must Break You."[1]

They are more than just words. Months earlier, Drago had not only broken Apollo Creed, but he had actually killed him in the ring! Now Rocky, standing almost a foot shorter than the giant Drago, must pull off the ultimate David vs. Goliath victory.

Rocky goes 15 rounds against the giant in an amazing act of valor, eventually knocking him out. It was a victory no one expected, a twist in the tale as Rocky, like a modern-day David, chopped down the enemy that wanted to destroy him.

Rocky took a beating, but he refused to be defeated. In the end, he stood victorious as an unbreakable boxer.

Men of God, we have an enemy that wants to break us. Satan wants to destroy us. He wants us in Hell with him at the end of the battle. He will throw everything he has at us throughout life to try and keep us away from God. He is vicious!

But as men of God, we can gain victory! All we need is available to us! We can gain victory against every attack.

The Bible promises us victory.

> *No weapon that is fashioned against you shall succeed, and you shall refute every tongue that rises against you in judgment. This is the heritage of the servants of the Lord and their vindication from me, declares the Lord. -Isaiah 54:17 (ESV)*

> *In all these things we are more than conquerors through him who loved us. -Romans 8:37 (ESV)*

These are just two of the many verses that tell us we can gain victory. But there is one thing you must remember: To win, you have to fight!

Rocky didn't gain victory by just taunting or talking. He had to fight, giving everything he had to the battle. He was bloodied, and he felt pain, but he fought with everything he had, and in the end, he stood victorious.

Too many men of God are running from the fight, or worse yet, just surrendering and settling for defeat.

Fight! Stand Firm! Give it everything you got! This is the attitude of an unbreakable man, and when he fights like this, he will gain victory.

The enemy wants to break you…will you run in fear or fight to victory?

SUNDAY

- [ ] Psalms 24-26

MONDAY

- [ ] Proverbs 26-27
- [ ] Matthew 25

TUESDAY

- [ ] Proverbs 28
- [ ] Matthew 26

WEDNESDAY

- [ ] Proverbs 29-30
- [ ] Matthew 27

THURSDAY

- [ ] Proverbs 31
- [ ] Matthew 28

FRIDAY

- [ ] Exodus 1-2
- [ ] Galatians 1

NOTES AND REFLECTION

MEMORY VERSE

Let us hold fast the confession of our hope without wavering, for He who promised is faithful. -Hebrews 10:23

WEEK TEN

LIFE IS TOO SHORT TO LEARN FROM YOUR OWN MISTAKES; LEARN FROM OTHER PEOPLE'S MISTAKES.
-VACATION HOUSE RULES

I admit it—I've become old! I have injured myself while sleeping. Leaving the house after nine p.m. seems like a crazy notion to me, and I enjoy watching HGTV! It's all downhill from here!

Of course, I joke; my best years are still ahead. But I am indeed getting older. And you know what? I'm loving every moment of it. It's also true that I enjoy home repair shows.

The quote we started this devotional with is from a show called *Vacation House Rules,* where they take rundown vacation houses and make them into beautiful retreats.

In one episode, two brothers in their early twenties asked the host to help them turn their rundown ranch into a vacation destination. But they went further. They said they not only wanted his help but also wanted him to teach them how to do what he did.

The host didn't get intimidated or territorial. Instead, he took the challenge and taught them how to do what he does.

He made them roll up their sleeves and work alongside him. As they worked, he told them why he was doing what he was doing and why it was the best way to achieve long-term results.

He truly exemplified his own words. *"Life is too short to learn from your own mistakes; learn from other people's mistakes."*[1]

What a great attitude. It is one we all must embrace in our lives.

I personally have benefitted from other men who have this attitude. Not wanting to see me fail, they shared their wisdom and experience of times they made mistakes and how I can avoid the same potholes in life.

I now try to do the same. I have made many mistakes in my life and suffered the consequences of these mistakes. Why would I want someone else to go through the same thing? If my mistakes can help others soar over the mistakes damage-free, I will happily be vulnerable and share my stupidity to help them.

Life really is too short, especially in God's Kingdom. Every minute not spent digging your way out of a mess can be used to grow God's kingdom.

An unbreakable man understands this and is willing to learn from other men's mistakes. He is also willing to share his mistakes with the next generation so they can avoid them. It takes being both teachable and vulnerable, but it is the heart of an unbreakable man!

SUNDAY
☐ Psalms 27-29

MONDAY
☐ Exodus 3-4

☐ Galatians 2

TUESDAY
☐ Exodus 5-6

☐ Galatians 3

WEDNESDAY
☐ Exodus 7-8

☐ Galatians 4

THURSDAY
☐ Exodus 9-10

☐ Galatians 5

FRIDAY
☐ Exodus 11-12

☐ Galatians 6

NOTES AND REFLECTION

MEMORY VERSE

Finally, be strong in the Lord and in the strength of his might. -Ephesians 6:10

WEEK ELEVEN

THE WORLD AIN'T ALL SUNSHINE AND RAINBOWS. IT IS A VERY MEAN AND NASTY PLACE AND IT WILL BEAT YOU TO YOUR KNEES AND KEEP YOU THERE PERMANENTLY IF YOU LET IT. YOU, ME, OR NOBODY IS GONNA HIT AS HARD AS LIFE. BUT IT AIN'T HOW HARD YOU HIT; IT'S ABOUT HOW HARD YOU CAN GET HIT, AND KEEP MOVING FORWARD. HOW MUCH YOU CAN TAKE, AND KEEP MOVING FORWARD. THAT'S HOW WINNING IS DONE.

NOW, IF YOU KNOW WHAT YOU'RE WORTH, THEN GO OUT AND GET WHAT YOU'RE WORTH. BUT YA GOTTA BE WILLING TO TAKE THE HITS, AND NOT POINTING FINGERS SAYING YOU AIN'T WHERE YOU ARE BECAUSE OF HIM, OR HER, OR ANYBODY. COWARDS DO THAT AND THAT AIN'T YOU. YOU'RE BETTER THAN THAT![1] - ROCKY, ROCKY BALBOA

In my humble opinion, this is the best quote from a *Rocky* movie! It is such a powerful quote, especially how they tie it back in at the end of the fight when Rocky struggles to stay in the fight. It is so powerful, and it is so applicable to an unbreakable man!

Life is filled with challenges that can test our faith and resolve. Rocky Balboa's words are a powerful reminder that the world isn't always a place of sunshine and rainbows. It's a tough place that can knock us down. It wants you to stay down, defeated, playing the victim. But as Christian men, we are called to be unbreakable, standing firm in our faith no matter how hard life hits us.

Jesus warned us that we would face tribulations in this world. Yet, He also assured us of His victory over the world.

> *I have told you all this so that you may have peace in me. Here on earth you will have many trials and sorrows. But take heart, because I have overcome the world. -John 16:33 (NLT)*

This victory is our strength and our foundation. When life hits hard, we can take those hits and keep moving forward because of our hope and strength in Christ. It is what defines us as unbreakable men of God.

Rocky's message emphasizes persistence and perseverance when he says, *"It ain't how hard you hit; it's about how hard you can get hit and keep moving forward."*[1]

In life, we are often tested, but our faith gives us the power to endure. We are not defined by the hits we take but by our response to those hits. And believe me, the hits and blows will come! But, with Christ, we can take the hardest blows and still stand strong, moving forward in His grace and strength.

An unbreakable man confidently takes responsibility for his issues and struggles. He doesn't play the victim or point fingers at others. It's easy to blame others for our struggles, but as Rocky points out, cowards do that. We are called to take ownership of our lives and actions. As unbreakable Christian men, we confidently look to God for our worth and strength, trusting in His plan and timing, knowing He will never abandon us.

Remember Rocky's words: Keep moving forward, persevere, and fight until you win.

This is the heart and mind of a victorious, unbreakable person!

SUNDAY
- [ ] Psalms 30-32

MONDAY
- [ ] Exodus 13-14
- [ ] Ephesians 1

TUESDAY
- [ ] Exodus 15-16
- [ ] Ephesians 2

WEDNESDAY
- [ ] Exodus 17-18
- [ ] Ephesians 3

THURSDAY
- [ ] Exodus 19-20
- [ ] Ephesians 4

FRIDAY
- [ ] Exodus 21-22
- [ ] Ephesians 5

NOTES AND REFLECTION

MEMORY VERSE

Put on the whole armor of God, that you may be able to stand against the schemes of the devil. -Ephesians 6:11

Week Twelve

FOLLOW MY EXAMPLE, AS I FOLLOW THE EXAMPLE OF CHRIST. -PAUL

Wow!

What a challenge from Paul in 1 Corinthians 11:1. It is bold, it is confident, and it is extremely, extremely scary!

Yet, it is a challenge we should all embrace. But to do so, we need to ask ourselves what kind of example we are leaving to follow. This self-examination is crucial in our journey of faith.

The model life of a man of God, the blueprint of how we should live, is one of mentorship and discipleship. It was Jesus's last command before He returned to His Heavenly Father: We are to go and make disciples. (Matthew 28:19-20)

Making disciples and mentoring someone else means you use your life as an example of how they should live. You are literally giving them a tour of manhood...mantour=mentor.

Our God-given responsibility is to live a life that younger men can observe and use as a model. They should see how we live and then try to go even further in their walk with God than we have. This is a weighty responsibility, but it is God's plan for man.

We are talking about heavy stuff here. It is life and death. It always needs to be at the front of our minds. If it were, I think fewer sins and fewer compromises would occur among God's men.

Paul's challenge reminds us to live our lives with purpose. We must remember that we don't run the race set before us for our personal gain but for the benefit of the next generation.

Just as we look to the great men of the Bible for guidance, the next generation looks to us for inspiration. Let's strive to set positive examples for them to follow.

So, how does this impact our lives?

I believe the key takeaway is that every decision we make, every path we choose, is being observed by others. Our spiritual journey and our walk with God are not hidden; instead, they are like glass houses where others can see and be influenced by our actions. It's important for us to regularly assess ourselves and ensure that we are setting a positive example for others to follow.

We must always remember that no man is an island, and how we live doesn't just affect our own lives; it influences countless other lives around us. If we keep this focus in our lives and commit to following God wholeheartedly with fervency and passion, rejecting sin and temptation while pursuing God's grace and will, we can walk forward and emulate Paul's sentiment: *"I'm following God. Watch me and follow God, too."*

SUNDAY
- [ ] Psalms 33-35

MONDAY
- [ ] Exodus 23-24
- [ ] Ephesians 6

TUESDAY
- [ ] Exodus 31-32
- [ ] Philippians 1

WEDNESDAY
- [ ] Exodus 33-34
- [ ] Philippians 2

THURSDAY
- [ ] Exodus 35-36
- [ ] Philippians 3

FRIDAY
- [ ] Exodus 40
- [ ] Philippians 4

NOTES AND REFLECTION

MEMORY VERSE

For we do not wrestle against flesh and blood, but against the rulers, against the authorities, against the cosmic powers over this present darkness, against the spiritual forces of evil in the heavenly places. -Ephesians 6:12

Week Thirteen

A HERO CAN BE ANYONE — EVEN A MAN DOING SOMETHING AS SIMPLE AND REASSURING AS PUTTING A COAT AROUND A YOUNG BOY'S SHOULDERS TO LET HIM KNOW THAT THE WORLD HADN'T ENDED.[1]
-BRUCE WAYNE, THE DARK KNIGHT RISES

Batman. The story of Bruce Wayne—a man with everything—money, fame, prestige, and power. Yet, as with all great origin stories, Batman is filled with tragedy. Haunted by the murder of his parents by the criminal element in Gotham, Bruce Wayne struggles with his own demons. No version shows this aspect of his life better than the Batman Trilogy starring Christian Bale.

In this series of movies, we meet Bruce Wayne as a child. We witnessed his parents' shooting as the family was going to the theatre. Later that night, we see Bruce Wayne as a petrified and grief-stricken child waiting in a police station.

That's when we meet another hero, Jim Gordon, at the beginning of his career as a police officer. Seeing the broken child, Officer Gordon kneels beside him and comforts him, placing a coat around his shoulders and telling him, *"It's going to be okay."*[2]

At that moment, we see the origin story of the two heroes in the *Dark Knight* series.

There is no doubt that there are two heroes in this story.

Obviously, there was the Dark Knight, Batman, a.k.a. Bruce Wayne, who determined he would use all of his wealth, genius, energy, and tech to fight crime and save Gotham City.

And yet, Batman was not the only hero in this series of movies.

Lt. James Gordon was also a hero. Even though he didn't wear a costume or a mask, his exploits were less glamorous; his equipment wasn't as high-tech and expensive. Lt. James Gordon spent every day fighting against the evil element in Gotham City and preserving justice. For decades, he stood against the powers of evil and did all he could to clean up the streets, protect the citizens, and keep Gotham from destroying itself. From within the system and often behind the scenes, Gordon fought the good fight for the city he loved.

That is why in *The Dark Knight Rises*, Batman tells Gordon, *"A hero can be anyone — even a man doing something as simple and reassuring as putting a coat around a young boy's shoulders to let him know that the world hadn't ended."*[1]

It was a moment that Bruce Wayne and Gordon shared, yet it was a story that many others could have also told. Undoubtedly, many others could have told similar stories where Officer Gordon proved to be a hero without all the glory and publicity of Batman's exploits.

In many ways, Officer Gordon represents many of God's men who quietly live heroic lives, taking care of the people around them.

He represents the men we don't hear about often enough.

The men who love God and do their best to serve Him.

The men who sacrifice for their families, who love their wives and kids. Those who raise their sons and daughters to walk in God's ways.

These men get up every morning, go to work for an honest day's pay, and represent Jesus the entire time. Then, they come home and serve their families, volunteer their time to coach the team, teach the class, lead the Royal Rangers, or help a neighbor.

They are the men who hold their churches together by doing the jobs that no one else wants to do. They make the repairs, fill in the gaps, visit people in hospitals, and pray at the altars.

They are the men holding communities together by serving on committees, filling out the paperwork for grants, fighting the fires, helping committees, and organizing events.

The man who sees the boy without a father, takes him under his wing…invites him to church…, and gets him involved in the youth group.

The man who sees a family struggling and drops off groceries.

The foster parent. The adoptive parent. The man who mentors others and shows them a better life.

These are the true heroes in our world—men who use their masculinity, strength, knowledge, and compassion to meet the needs of others.

Those who live by Micah 6:8:

> *He has told you, O man, what is good; and what does the Lord require of you but to do justice, and to love kindness, and to walk humbly with your God? (ESV)*

Even though they may not wear a mask or a cape, they can't fly, and they don't have superpowers, the men who serve God and others daily are the true heroes. They are the men who change the world.

SUNDAY
- [ ] Psalms 36-38

MONDAY
- [ ] Numbers 9-10
- [ ] Colossians 1

TUESDAY
- [ ] Numbers 11-12
- [ ] Colossians 2

WEDNESDAY
- [ ] Numbers 13-14
- [ ] Colossians 3

THURSDAY
- [ ] Numbers 16-17
- [ ] Colossians 4

FRIDAY
- [ ] Numbers 20-21
- [ ] Philemon 1

NOTES AND REFLECTION

MEMORY VERSE

Therefore take up the whole armor of God, that you may be able to withstand in the evil day, and having done all, to stand firm.
-Ephesians 6:13

Week Fourteen

I'M NOT GOING ANYWHERE. I'M LIKE THE STINK ON YOUR FEET, I'LL ALWAYS BE AROUND. [1]
-BEDTIME STORIES

I love this quote! In the movie *Bedtime Stories*, Adam Sandler is tasked with watching his niece and nephew for a week while their mom is out of town looking for a job. While he watches them, he makes up a bedtime story to tell them every night. Throughout the movie, we see him become closer and more attached to his niece and nephew.

One night, his niece, whose father had recently deserted them, asked if her uncle thought her dad would ever come back. What a heartbreaking question. He answered her that they would always have their mother, and then he added, *"I'm not going anywhere. I'm like the stink on your feet; I'll always be around."*[1]

What an amazing line! It's humorous but clearly communicates that he will always be there for them. He won't abandon them; he will always support and stand by them.

So many today know what it's like to be abandoned. Fatherlessness is a massive problem in the world. According to the 2022 U.S. Census, approximately 18.3 million children live without a father in the home, comprising about one out of four U.S. children.[2]

Many who grew up without a father and have known the pain of abandonment really struggle with seeing God as their Father. They expect God, like their earthly dad, will leave them. He won't be there for them. He will abandon them and leave them high and dry.

They are ok with seeing God as their Lord. They know they need Him as their Savior. But Father, heck no!

As men of God, we must realize that God will never abandon us. He is with us every minute of every day. We have His word that He will never leave us or forsake us. He will always be there for us.

Hebrews 13:5-6 clearly says, *"I will never leave you nor forsake you." So we can confidently say, "The Lord is my helper; I will not fear; what can man do to me?" (ESV)*

God will always be there for you, no matter what your earthly father did. He will never leave you or forsake you. He will always be around.

An unbreakable man knows that he can rely on God. God has your back.

Just as Adam Sandler's character reassured his niece and nephew that he would always be there for them, it is comforting to know that we have a heavenly Father who will never leave us.

Despite any past experiences, we can find comfort in God's unchanging love and support. His presence in our lives is constant, providing us with the strength and assurance we need to navigate life's challenges. Like the stink on our feet, God will always be around, ready to guide, comfort, and support us.

SUNDAY
- [ ] Psalms 40-42

MONDAY
- [ ] Numbers 22-23
- [ ] John 1

TUESDAY
- [ ] Numbers 24-25
- [ ] John 2

WEDNESDAY
- [ ] Numbers 27, 31
- [ ] John 3

THURSDAY
- [ ] Numbers 32-33
- [ ] John 4

FRIDAY
- [ ] Joshua 1-2
- [ ] John 5

NOTES AND REFLECTION

MEMORY VERSE

Stand therefore, having fastened on the belt of truth, and having put on the breastplate of righteousness, and, as shoes for your feet, having put on the readiness given by the gospel of peace. -Ephesians 6:14-15

Week Fifteen

CREATE IN ME A CLEAN HEART, O GOD, AND RENEW A RIGHT SPIRIT WITHIN ME. CAST ME NOT AWAY FROM YOUR PRESENCE, AND TAKE NOT YOUR HOLY SPIRIT FROM ME. RESTORE TO ME THE JOY OF YOUR SALVATION, AND UPHOLD ME WITH A WILLING SPIRIT. -KING DAVID

He was down for the count.

The great King David, the slayer of giants, the man after God's own heart, had sinned. The leader of Israel broke two of the Ten Commandments.

> *You shall not murder. You shall not commit adultery.*
> *-Exodus 20:13-14 (ESV)*

His lustful eyes caused him to sin. When Bathsheba became pregnant, he killed her husband to cover it up.

How did David respond when Nathan the prophet showed up and said, *"God knows, and He isn't pleased?"*

> *Nathan said to David, "You are the man! Thus says the Lord, the God of Israel, 'I anointed you king over Israel, and I delivered you out of the hand of Saul. And I gave you your master's house and your master's wives into your arms and gave you the house of Israel and of Judah. And if this were too little, I would add to you as much more. Why have you despised the word of the Lord, to do what is evil in*

his sight? You have struck down Uriah the Hittite with the sword and have taken his wife to be your wife and have killed him with the sword of the Ammonites.

Now therefore the sword shall never depart from your house, because you have despised me and have taken the wife of Uriah the Hittite to be your wife.'

Thus says the Lord, 'Behold, I will raise up evil against you out of your own house. And I will take your wives before your eyes and give them to your neighbor, and he shall lie with your wives in the sight of this sun.

For you did it secretly, but I will do this thing before all Israel and before the sun.'" -2 Samuel 12:7-12 (ESV)

King David had sinned and was broken. But what he did next sets the example for all men who have fallen into sin but want to become unbreakable again.

What did he do? He repented.

David said to Nathan, "I have sinned against the Lord." -2 Samuel 12:13 (ESV)

Psalm 51 is the exact words that David prayed after he faced his sin. That's where we see the quote:

Create in me a clean heart, O God, and renew a right spirit within me.

Cast me not away from your presence, and take not your Holy Spirit from me.

Restore to me the joy of your salvation, and uphold me with a willing spirit. -Psalm 51:10-12 (ESV)

What do you do when you fall into sin?

Well, the first thing you need to do is admit that you sinned. You need to stop excusing what you did. Stop playing around with it and acting like it's no big deal.

Then, we must do what David did and ask God to forgive us.

We need to recognize, as Joseph did, that all sin is ultimately against God and sincerely ask Him to forgive us. You might even want to pray Psalm 51.

However, true repentance doesn't end with just saying *"sorry."* True repentance means that you change.

No, change isn't always easy, but true repentance does whatever it takes to change your behavior—to stop sinning. Repentance means turning around and going in the opposite direction.

Here's the amazing part: **when you decide to do everything you can to remove sin from your life, the Holy Spirit inside you partners with you to give you the strength to do everything you can't do on your own.**

When your continued determination partners with the power of the Holy Spirit, together you can overcome any sin, restore your relationship with God, and do the work necessary to fix your relationship with others and your reputation.

The truth is that no man is too broken to experience God's forgiveness and healing and start a new life.

But the key is to humble yourself before God in repentance, ask for forgiveness, and partner with the Holy Spirit to stop sinning.

To admit, like David did, I have sinned, but I don't want this to be the end of my story.

SUNDAY
- [ ] Psalms 43-45

MONDAY
- [ ] Joshua 3-4
- [ ] John 6

TUESDAY
- [ ] Joshua 5-6
- [ ] John 7

WEDNESDAY
- [ ] Joshua 7-8
- [ ] John 8

THURSDAY
- [ ] Joshua 9-10
- [ ] John 9

FRIDAY
- [ ] Joshua 11-12
- [ ] John 10

NOTES AND REFLECTION

MEMORY VERSE

In all circumstances take up the shield of faith, with which you can extinguish all the flaming darts of the evil one; -Ephesians 6:16

Week Sixteen

GOD PROVED HIS LOVE ON THE CROSS. WHEN CHRIST HUNG AND BLED, AND DIED, IT WAS GOD SAYING TO THE WORLD, "I LOVE YOU."[1] -BILLY GRAHAM

As men, we often feel the need to prove our strength, protect those we care about, and earn the respect of others. We all have an inner Rodney Dangerfield telling us, *"I get no respect!"*[2] We work and try to gain respect constantly.

We strive to be reliable, stand firm in our commitments, and love fiercely. But no matter how hard we try, there are times when we fall short. Life hits us between the eyes, and we are flat on the mat. In those moments, it's easy to feel unworthy, unloved, and distant from God.

Billy Graham's words remind us of a powerful truth: God's love isn't something we have to earn. It's a gift freely given, proven once and for all on the cross. When Christ hung, bled, and died, it wasn't just a display of sacrifice—it was the ultimate declaration of love from God to you, a love that is unconditional and unwavering.

This love is not based on our performance, successes, or failures. It's rooted in God's character, unfailing grace, and desire to have a relationship with us. Christ didn't wait for us to clean up our act, to be good enough before He extended His love. He died for us while we were still sinners—down on the mat, defeated and broken.

God's love transforms us. This love calls us back to God when we fall into temptation or sin. This love forgives us when we fall and strengthens us to begin again.

As men, we are called to reflect this love in our lives. We should love our families, friends, and even our enemies, not because they deserve it but because God has loved us. We didn't deserve God's love, so we can't make others feel they must earn our love. We know God reached down and picked us up off the mat, and we, in turn, extend our hand to help others who have been knocked down. This kind of love is patient, kind, and selfless. It's the love that builds up rather than tears down.

This week, as we celebrate the resurrection of Jesus from the grave, conquering death and hell and reuniting us with God, we must take a moment to reflect on the love of God displayed on the cross.

This reflection should inspire us to show the same love to those around us. Whether through an act of kindness, a word of encouragement, or simply being there for someone in need, let the love of Christ be evident in all you do. An unbreakable man shows God's love to those around them and makes a difference in the lives of others because he knows God did it for him first.

SUNDAY
☐ **Psalms 46-48**

MONDAY
☐ **Joshua 14-16**

☐ **John 11**

TUESDAY
☐ **Joshua 20, 22**

☐ **John 12**

WEDNESDAY
☐ **Joshua 23-24**

☐ **John 13**

THURSDAY
☐ **Ruth 1-2**

☐ **John 14**

FRIDAY
☐ **Ruth 3-4**

☐ **John 15**

NOTES AND REFLECTION

MEMORY VERSE

Take the helmet of salvation, and the sword of the Spirit, which is the word of God.
-Ephesians 6:17

Week Seventeen

GET UP KID![1] -ROCKY

I love that the *Rocky* franchise continued into the *Creed* Franchise!

While *Creed* was a fantastic movie, I thought *Creed II* was even better. It starts with Adonis Creed, coached by Rocky Balboa, winning the heavyweight title. But then he faces a challenge from both his and Rocky's past.

Ivan Drago's son challenges Creed to a fight.

Remember, Ivan Drago killed Apollo Creed in the ring. Now, his son was challenging Donnie. Adonis takes the fight and gets beaten to a pulp. It's bad. He spends weeks in the hospital. He is wounded, but even worse, his spirit is crushed.

Donnie continues with his life but never moves on from being laid out on the mat. He won't fight. He won't train. Eventually, Rocky gets through to him, and Donnie agrees to a rematch. After one of the most epic training montages in a *Rocky* movie (more on this in a later devotional), Adonis is ready and enters the ring for a rematch. It goes well for him through the first few rounds, but the fight turns around in round 9, and Donnie gets pummeled again.

Viktor Drago lands blow after blow against Donnie, and he eventually gives him the roundhouse that sends Donnie to the mat. Donnie is down, and he looks like he is out.

As he struggles to get back to his feet, he sees his wife and mom yelling for him to get up. He hears Rocky say, *"Get up, kid."*[1] He looks around, weak and unable to stand.

Then, we see something inside of him change. He punches his fist to the mat, then his other fist. He punches the mat over and over. At that moment, he gets mad! He gets tired of being knocked down. He gets angry at feeling weak and defeated. He punches the mat, and he stands to his feet.

He got back up. Drago looked at him in stunned disbelief that he had gotten back up after such a beating! Donnie went at Drago with every ounce of strength and determination he had, eventually knocking him down and winning the fight.

Donnie had to make a choice. Would he stay defeated and on the mat, or would he get back up and fight?

Guys, many of you are down on the mat. The enemy has knocked you down over and over. For some of you, it was a recent defeat; for others, you have been down and out for weeks, months, and even years. Like Adonis, you are beaten, bleeding spiritually, and you don't know what to do.

It is time for you to get angry…punch the mat, get mad at your current state, and find the resolve to fight. Get up off the mat!

Adonis looked around at his family for encouragement. They all said, *"Get up!"*

Guys, you have family and friends all around you who want to see you crawl out of bed and get back up. They want you to gain victory. They want you to get up.

You need to punch that mat and resolve to get up and fight.

In the movie, when Donnie gets up, the ref asks him his name, and he yells, *"Creed!"*

In your fight, the enemy will ask you who you think you are. Why do you think you can fight? Who do you think you are to get back up and face off again?

When he asks, you scream, *"I am a child of GOD!"*

You have everything you need to rise off your knees, wipe the blood off your chin and the sweat off your brow, and get back into the fight.

Are you ready to punch the mat and get back up?

The Bible tells us that the righteous man falls seven times, but he gets back up. (Proverbs 24:16)

Don't let yourself fall prey to the enemy's lies that you are hopeless and can never gain victory. He is a liar! John 8:44 says he is the father of lies. STOP BELIEVING HIM!

Grace, forgiveness, and victory await you from your Heavenly Father. He does not condemn you; He forgives. You may need to face consequences for your sins, but He will walk with you as you deal with them. He is your loving Father Who wants to see you gain victory.

You have been down for too long. Your sin knocked you down to the mat, and you stayed there too long. It seems impossible to get up and start again. You feel there is no point; you will just end up back where you are now. But it is time to get up!

SUNDAY
☐ Psalms 49-51

MONDAY
☐ Judges 1-2

☐ John 16

TUESDAY
☐ Judges 3-4

☐ John 17

WEDNESDAY
☐ Judges 5-6

☐ John 18

THURSDAY
☐ Judges 7-8

☐ John 19

FRIDAY
☐ Judges 9-10

☐ John 20

NOTES AND REFLECTION

MEMORY VERSE

God, the Lord, is my strength; he makes my feet like the deer's; he makes me tread on my high places. -Habakkuk 3:19

Week Eighteen

IF YOU WANT TO CHANGE THINGS IN A BIG WAY, YOU NEED TO MAKE SOME BIG CHANGES. -ROCKY, CREED II

In the movie *Creed II*, Adonis Creed ignores Rocky's advice and takes a fight against the son of the man who killed his father, Apollo. As Rocky warned, the fight is a disaster. Donnie gets destroyed by Viktor Drago. He gets beaten so severely that he is in the hospital for weeks. But worse than the physical beating, the fight leaves Donnie a broken man.

He is mentally destroyed, unable to fight and find his way back into the ring. He appears to be down for the count.

Then something beautiful happens. Rocky comes and makes Donnie face his fears. He makes him see what is going on. Then, he offers a helping hand to help him up off the mental, defeated mat Donnie is living on.

What follows is one of the greatest training montages in film history. Rocky knows that if Donnie beats Drago in a rematch, he has to become unbreakable. So he takes him to the desert to a fight camp where fighters go to start over. In Rocky's words, *"If you want to change things in a big way, you need to make some big changes. "*[1]

I love that line! Too many broken men never get unbroken because they keep going down the same path, make the same choices, and fall into the same sinful patterns. They stay broken because they don't do the work necessary to change. They do the same things, hoping for different results, but all that ends up happening is they get knocked on their butts again.

We cannot gain victory if we don't make changes in our lives. It's insane to think you can win using the same tactics in the battle as you did last time you fell into sin. Yet daily, men of God do just this.

Creed had to make big changes. He had to learn to take a beating, get tough, strengthen his core, endure, and never give up or stop fighting. Defeat was no longer an option. No matter how hard the punch, he had to stand. And if he got knocked down, he had to get back up and fight again.

Guys, you must do the same to become an unbreakable man.

Identify what caused you to lose in the past, and then do the opposite.

If you struggle with porn late at night, set a lock on your devices so you can't access it.

If you are flying off the handle when someone challenges you or questions you, start examining yourself and discover why. Then, do the opposite and accept the correction.

Do you struggle with lying and deceit? Vow only to speak honestly and truth, no matter the cost.

Newton (the scientist, not the fig guy) had a point when he said, *"For every action, there is an equal and opposite reaction."* [2]

If your normal way of acting and living isn't leading to victory, it's time for a new plan of attack and a new way of living. While it may be scary, it is key to becoming an unbreakable man of God who settles for nothing less than living a victorious life.

SUNDAY
☐ Psalms 52-54

MONDAY
☐ Judges 11-12

☐ John 21

TUESDAY
☐ Judges 13-14

☐ Acts 1

WEDNESDAY
☐ Judges 15-16

☐ Acts 2

THURSDAY
☐ Judges 17-18

☐ Acts 3

FRIDAY
☐ Judges 19-21

☐ Acts 4

NOTES AND REFLECTION

MEMORY VERSE

God gave us a spirit not of fear but of power and love and self-control. -2 Timothy 1:7

Week Nineteen

A MAN'S GOT TO HAVE A CODE, A CREED TO LIVE BY, NO MATTER HIS JOB. –JOHN WAYNE[1]

What would a devotional based on great quotes be without a quote by John Wayne?

The Duke, as he was known, was a man's man, an actor with iconic movie roles in which he played cowboys, soldiers, police officers, an oil well fire repairman, and many more.

These words spoken by the Duke ring true today. All men need a code to live by, follow, and live out daily. An unbreakable man has such a code! His code is the Word of God!

I firmly believe that men of God need to be men of the Word. It must be our code.

It is the lamp to our feet and light to our path (Psalm 119:105).

It is the moral authority we follow. It is God's book of instruction, our user manual for life.

An unbreakable man is known as a man who reads God's Word. But he goes further than that. He allows it to change him. He lets the Holy Spirit convict him, showing him areas to change and be more like Jesus.

The words in the Bible start to define such a man. He measures truth and lies against God's Word. He discerns attacks and temptations because he knows what God's Word says. He uses the Word of God as a weapon to fight back against the enemy's attack.

Such a man prioritizes reading the Bible. He knows salvation isn't earned by time spent in the Word; salvation only comes by grace and faith in God. But he recognizes that the Bible will keep him strong and unwavering, revealing the best way to live, act, and believe.

The unbreakable man knows the Word of God is all-powerful and never-changing. He embraces it as his life code and strives to live it out daily.

Men, let's take inspiration from John Wayne's words and strive to live by a code grounded in the timeless wisdom of the Word of God. May we be unbreakable in our commitment to reading, understanding, and living out the teachings of the Bible, allowing it to shape us into men of unwavering faith and resilience. As we face life's challenges, may the Word of God be our guide, source of strength, and ultimate code for living a purposeful and fulfilling life.

SUNDAY
- [ ] Psalms 55-57

MONDAY
- [ ] Ezra 1-2
- [ ] Acts 5

TUESDAY
- [ ] Ezra 3-4
- [ ] Acts 6

WEDNESDAY
- [ ] Ezra 5-6
- [ ] Acts 7

THURSDAY
- [ ] Ezra 7-8
- [ ] Acts 8

FRIDAY
- [ ] Ezra 9-10
- [ ] Acts 9

NOTES AND REFLECTION

MEMORY VERSE

This Book of the Law shall not depart from your mouth, but you shall meditate on it day and night, so that you may be careful to do according to all that is written in it. For then you will make your way prosperous, and then you will have good success. -Joshua 1:8

Week Twenty

DON'T POINT THE FINGER, PULL THE THUMB.
-MARK SCHLERETH

I recently heard these words on a podcast hosted by Super Bowl Champion Mark Schlereth. Mark is a former Denver Broncos offensive lineman and currently a play-by-play analyst for the NFL on Fox. Most importantly, he is a fellow follower of Christ.

His point with this quote is that we often blame other people for our own problems and issues. We pass the buck, make excuses, and reflect our shortcomings on others. We do everything except the one thing that will help us become unbreakable men: we pull our thumbs at ourselves and say, *"You know who needs to change? This guy."*

Guys, we can't blame everyone else for our problems. While other people may cause some of the problems, it is our fault for allowing them to remain in our lives.

When I was younger, I struggled with many sins and issues that I either learned from my father or were the result of his abusive behavior toward me. Instead of facing them, I often felt sorry for myself and held onto anger and resentment towards him. Change didn't come until I realized that I had my own problems.

I couldn't keep excusing my behavior and blaming my dad. I had to get my eyes off of him and onto myself. I needed to stop saying, *"My dad was abusive,"* and start saying, *"I have a problem, and I need help."* I had to admit my faults, repent, and acknowledge that I needed to take responsibility for my actions.

Then, I had to start working on myself.

I couldn't change my father, but I could become a different man. I could allow the Holy Spirit to convict me and change me.

I could start living, thinking, and acting differently. But it wasn't possible until I stopped pointing the finger and pulled the thumb.

Proverbs 28:13 says, *"Whoever conceals his transgressions will not prosper, but he who confesses and forsakes them will obtain mercy." (ESV)*

Another way to say this is in Mark Schlereth's words: *"Stop pointing the finger and pull the thumb."*[1]

You become an unbreakable person only when you discover freedom and forgiveness and when change occurs.

SUNDAY

- [ ] Psalms 58-60

MONDAY

- [ ] Nehemiah 1-2
- [ ] Acts 10

TUESDAY

- [ ] Nehemiah 4-5
- [ ] Acts 11

WEDNESDAY

- [ ] Nehemiah 6-7
- [ ] Acts 12

THURSDAY

- [ ] Nehemiah 8-9, 10:28-37
- [ ] Acts 13

FRIDAY

- [ ] Nehemiah 12:27-47, 13
- [ ] Acts 14

NOTES AND REFLECTION

MEMORY VERSE

Have I not commanded you? Be strong and courageous. Do not be frightened, and do not be dismayed, for the Lord your God is with you wherever you go. -Joshua 1:9

Week Twenty-One

HERE I AM, LORD, SEND ME. -ISAIAH 6:8

This quote comes from Isaiah 6:8, when Isaiah *heard the voice of the Lord saying, "Whom shall I send, and who will go for us?"*

Isaiah replied, *"Here I am! Send me."* (ESV)

Often, when we hear a sermon about this Scripture or read a devotional using this verse, many men start to panic and think, *"What will I do if God calls me to leave everything and go and be a missionary in Africa?"*

"What if the Holy Spirit asks me to quit the job that I love and become a pastor?"

"What if this is the moment God calls me into full-time ministry?"

For some reading this book, that may be possible because God calls men of all ages, cultures, and backgrounds to leave everything behind, just like the disciples left their fishing nets and followed Him.

If God is calling you into full-time ministry, then, yes, it is your responsibility, honor, and privilege to respond like Isaiah and say, *"Here I am, Lord, send me."* What an adventure you will begin!

However, in this devotional, I'd like to take a moment and ask the question, *"What if that isn't what this phrase means for you?"*

What if God isn't calling you to leave everything, start all over, go to Bible college, and then into full-time ministry?

What if God is asking you:

• Who can I send to teach the young boys in Royal Rangers?

- Who can I send to help in the nursery?

- Who can I ask to give up their leisurely Saturday and rake leaves or do carpentry at the church?

What will your answer be?

Have you ever watched the TV scene where everyone is standing in a line, and someone asks for a volunteer?

Suddenly, everyone in the line stepped backward, leaving the one poor guy in the front who didn't move, saying, *"Oh man, I guess I'm stuck with the job."*

What if God is calling you to be the unbreakable man everyone can count on, someone who doesn't get stuck with the job but volunteers for it?

What if God wants you to volunteer for the job no one sees and very few want—the dirty job that will probably go on to be unrecognized?

When the need arises, will you answer, ***"Here I am, Lord, send me?"***

What if God is calling you to give to a missionary or an organization that stops sex trafficking? When the call goes out, and God says, *"I need people to support my kingdom financially,"* what do you say?

What if God asks you to lead a discipleship group for young men?

What if God calls you and your wife to be foster parents?

Are you open to the possibilities?

I know a man and his wife who are retired military. While neither feel called to full-time ministry, almost everyone in their church relies on them for some form of help. They even help Mantour Ministries by repairing our van for free and lifting things I can't with my disability. Yet, they most modeled Isaiah's answer when a young man in their youth group needed a home, so they invited them to stay with them. They gave him a family and structure, provided for his needs, and taught him how to live. They are making a phenomenal difference in his life because when the need was presented, they said, *"Here I am, send me!"*

I truly believe this: the church of God did not survive for over two thousand years because of the work of people on the stage or behind a pulpit. While these roles are essential and honored, the church of Jesus Christ has survived and thrived because of everyday men and women who had an unbreakable commitment to answer, ***"Here I am, Lord, send me"*** when they are asked to do the jobs that nobody else wanted to do.

Will you be one of these unbreakable men?

SUNDAY

☐ Psalms 61-63

MONDAY

☐ Esther 1-2

☐ Acts 15

TUESDAY

☐ Esther 3-4

☐ Acts 16

WEDNESDAY

☐ Esther 5-6

☐ Acts 17

THURSDAY

☐ Esther 7-8

☐ Acts 18

FRIDAY

☐ Esther 9-10

☐ Acts 19

NOTES AND REFLECTION

MEMORY VERSE

I have fought the good fight, I have finished the race, I have kept the faith. Henceforth there is laid up for me the crown of righteousness, which the Lord, the righteous judge, will award to me on that day, and not only to me but also to all who have loved his appearing. -2 Timothy 4:7-8

Week Twenty-Two

WHEN YOU DON'T HAVE TO WORK SO HARD, THEN QUIT WORKING SO HARD. -NICOLE CURTIS, REHAB ADDICT RESCUE

"Another quote from a home improvement show? Wow, you really do like HGTV!"

I sure do, and when I heard the host, Nicole Curtis, say these words, I instantly wrote them down.

Nicole was speaking to a man who had started his own business. They were discussing how hard it is to get things off the ground. She could relate to the guy because she, too, had spent years working on building her home renovation company.

As they talked, she mentioned to the guy that there would be a point when it wouldn't be necessary to work as hard as he does now. Long overtime hours would settle into an established working schedule. She then made the point we quoted at the beginning.

"When you don't have to work so hard, then quit working so hard."[1]

What she was saying was that when work becomes less, take the extra time and spend it with your family. Leave work at work; don't just keep working because you are used to it.

Many people, especially men, derive their purpose and identity from what they do. Their self-esteem is derived from their work. They base who they are on what they do. Because of this, they often push hard at the expense of their family and personal lives.

Solomon wrote in Ecclesiastes 3:1-2, *"For everything there is a season, and a time for every matter under heaven...a time to plant, and a time to pluck up what is planted." (ESV)*

The time to work hard and build a career is important. But eventually, that season should lessen, and you can start to reap the benefits of this work.

I'm not talking about retirement. I'm talking about everyday life. A personal example may explain it.

When we started Mantour Ministries, I had to work my tail off to get these conferences going. I had to make calls, advertise, figure out how to do things, plan, budget, and so many other things. It was not uncommon for me to work 60 hours a week, work on holidays, and put all my efforts into starting this ministry.

I gained a lot of self-esteem from my hard work. People always praised my hard work and effort, and I enjoyed this praise. My job became my identity. Then, one day, my mentor told me I was working so hard that I was missing life. He spoke a word I desperately needed to hear…BALANCE.

Now, I'd love to say that I instantly changed and became Mr. Balance. But I didn't. COVID hit shortly after that, and there wasn't anything else to do, so I worked a lot.

Then I heard this woman say what we quoted above, and it hit me. I had to make sure that I started not working as hard. I'm not saying I don't work. I do…and I work hard when I work. But it doesn't take as much work to do what I do now as it used to; the simple fact of muscle memory and an organized system frees up time. So I work, but I also live. I have a life away from the office. I have found balance. I'm still working on it, but I am really trying not to let what I do define who I am.

Guys, an unstoppable man realizes that sometimes he must slow down and take a breath before moving forward. Balance.

It's okay to not always be working. It's okay to leave work at work and invest in your family. Give them what they deserve.

SUNDAY
- [ ] Psalms 64-66

MONDAY
- [ ] Jonah 1
- [ ] Acts 20-21

TUESDAY
- [ ] Jonah 2
- [ ] Acts 22-23

WEDNESDAY
- [ ] Jonah 3
- [ ] Acts 24-25

THURSDAY
- [ ] Jonah 4
- [ ] Acts 26-27

FRIDAY
- [ ] Obadiah 1
- [ ] Acts 28

NOTES AND REFLECTION

MEMORY VERSE

In all these things we are more than conquerors through him who loved us. -Romans 8:37

Week Twenty-Three

I FIGHT SO YOU DON'T HAVE TO FIGHT. -ROCKY IV

One of the most popular movies ever made for men is *Rocky IV*. When I talk about Rocky with other men, 75% say *Rocky IV* is their favorite *Rocky* movie. (My favorite is *Rocky III*, but *Rocky IV* is a close second!)

It is capitalism vs. communism, David vs. Goliath, good vs. evil. It is one of the best fights in movie history. IT IS EPIC!

But before all the fights, blood, death, and victory, there is a line that I love. Rocky is washing his beloved sports car, and his son asks him when he can learn to fight.

Rocky stops what he's doing, looks at his son, and says, *"I fight, so you don't have to fight. I want you to use your head for something other than a punching bag like I do."*[1]

Rocky fights to provide a better life for his son, a path to a better future. He wants his son to be able to learn and do whatever he wants to do. He doesn't want him to face the same beatings and defeats he faced. He doesn't want his son to get knocked out. He wants him to thrive in life.

This is an attitude that all unbreakable men of God need to adopt in their lives. We need to be willing to fight spiritual battles and gain victory so that the next generation doesn't have to face the same battles.

We fight and defeat addiction so it doesn't go to another generation.

We win the fight against porn so the next generation doesn't get trapped.

We defeat our anger issues so the next generation doesn't wrestle with the same anger.

Whatever the struggle, an unbreakable man fights to gain freedom and victory, not just for his own spiritual blessing, but to clear the battlefield for the next generation.

Exodus 20:5-6 says it clearly:

> *I the Lord your God am a jealous God, visiting the iniquity of the fathers on the children to the third and the fourth generation of those who hate me, but showing steadfast love to thousands of those who love me and keep my commandments. -Exodus 20:5-6 (ESV)*

God blesses the descendants of a righteous man for a thousand generations when he defeats his enemies and gains victory. Like Rocky, we don't just fight for ourselves. We fight so the next generation doesn't have to fight.

Are you doing everything you can to gain victory, or do you keep playing around with pet sins?

Do you want your children and grandchildren to struggle like you?

Will you do what is necessary to gain victory so they don't have to?

This is the heart of an unbreakable man. Get in the fight!

The powerful messages from the movie *Rocky IV* and Exodus 20:5-6 highlight the critical importance of fighting our battles to secure a better future for the next generation. We must strive to overcome our own struggles, not just for our benefit but also to pave a victorious path for those who come after us. It is a call to action for all of us to take responsibility for our actions and strive to lead by example, creating a legacy of strength, resilience, and victory for future generations. As an unbreakable man, commit to fighting for a better tomorrow.

SUNDAY
☐ Psalms 67-69

MONDAY
☐ 1 Samuel 1-2

☐ 1 Thessalonians 1

TUESDAY
☐ 1 Samuel 3-4

☐ 1 Thessalonians 2

WEDNESDAY
☐ 1 Samuel 5-6

☐ 1 Thessalonians 3

THURSDAY
☐ 1 Samuel 7-8

☐ 1 Thessalonians 4

FRIDAY
☐ 1 Samuel 9-10

☐ 1 Thessalonians 5

NOTES AND REFLECTION

MEMORY VERSE

He gives power to the faint, and to him who has no might he increases strength. -Isaiah 40:29

Week Twenty-Four

BUILD YOUR OWN LEGACY .[1] MA! -MARY ANNE CREED

These words were written on the note inside the gift Mary Anne sent Adonis Creed before his fight.

The gift reiterated the sentiment. It was his father, Apollo Creed's boxing shorts with the name *Creed* on the front but his name *Johnson* on the back.

The message was clear—fight and win the battle for yourself.

If you've ever seen *Creed*, you know this was a challenge for Adonis (Donnie).

Born the illegitimate son of the great boxer Apollo Creed, young Donnie had a lot going on inside him.

He wanted to live up to his father's reputation as a boxer, yet he was angry at his father for dying and leaving him alone. Most of all, as he told Rocky near the end of the fight, he needed to prove to himself and the world that he wasn't a mistake. Emotionally, the dude was a mess.

And yet, aren't we all at some point in our lives?

While few of us will ever have the chance to fight in a championship boxing match, we all struggle to fight the demons that plague us from our past.

For some, the pain and heartache of their past is unbearable. Whether consciously or unconsciously, they live their lives trying to overcome the pain of rejection, abandonment, trauma, or abuse. We live in a fatherless society, and many men carry deep wounds from their relationship or lack of relationship with their dad.

Others came from amazing families with great fathers. Often, these men struggle and wonder if they will ever be able to live up to the example of their parents.

No matter which side of the pendulum you live, or even if you fall somewhere in between, there comes a point where we all need to hear the words *"Build your own legacy."*

Here are some truths:

No man is destined to repeat their father's mistakes.

Through the power of the Holy Spirit, you can become your own person. You can be healed of the pain of your past, and you can become a completely new person made in the image of Christ rather than the image of your earthly father.

No matter who your father was—whether he was an abuser, an alcoholic, an inmate, an angry man, a man who left, or any other type of man who hurt you and his family—you are not destined to follow in his footsteps.

You can choose a different path because of the changing power of salvation and the Holy Spirit living in your life.

You can live as an unbreakable man of God and start a new legacy for yourself and your family.

On the other hand, **just because your father was a godly man or did extraordinary things does not mean that you are destined to live a life in his shadows.** Your calling is greater than simply trying to fill someone else's shoes.

Your identity is not just being someone's son—it comes from being God's son. God's plan for your life may be totally different from His plan for your father's life. He may call you to go further in life than your Dad did, or He may call you to walk in a completely different direction altogether.

Recently, I started watching a new show called *Cake Dynasty with Buddy Valastro*—the Cake Boss. I watched his first show, *Cake Boss,* many years ago on TLC. Back then, his children were babies, and the entire business occurred in a small business in Hoboken, NJ. I'm unsure if that show went off the air, or I just got bored. Either way, it has been at least a decade since I watched it.

Now he's back with a new show, and everything is different. First, his kids (the babies and toddlers in the first) are grown and working in the bakery. The business has grown, too. They now have bakeries and restaurants all over the country. Instead of working from a basement, the main headquarters is now a factory. It's a massive change.

Still, in almost every episode, Buddy talks about doing things the same way his father taught him to do them. He means he's still using the same recipes, still dedicated to quality, and working hard just like his Dad taught him. Yet, each time, I think, *"Let's be honest, there's nothing here like your dad did things."* All of the expansion brought massive changes.

The Holy Spirit has used this example to speak to my heart as I've been watching. He showed me that just like Buddy's business couldn't grow if he'd done everything exactly like his Dad did in the small family bakery, sometimes we need to let go of the *"way we've always done things"* or *"the way someone else did things"* so that we can grow and follow God's will for our lives.

The fact is that all growth necessitates change.

Change doesn't mean you disrespect or do not appreciate those who have come before.

Neither does admitting that those who came before us had struggles they didn't overcome in their lives.

It just means that, like Buddy, the Cake Boss, you are taking the foundation they gave you and building on it. You're taking their seed and allowing it to grow and expand.

You're building your legacy—being the man God created you to be and fulfilling His unique call for your life.

SUNDAY
☐ Psalms 70-72

MONDAY
☐ 1 Samuel 11-12

☐ 2 Thessalonians 1

TUESDAY
☐ 1 Samuel 13-14

☐ 2 Thessalonians 2

WEDNESDAY
☐ 1 Samuel 15-16

☐ 2 Thessalonians 3

THURSDAY
☐ 1 Samuel 17-18

☐ 1 Timothy 1

FRIDAY
☐ 1 Samuel 19-20

☐ 1 Timothy 2

NOTES AND REFLECTION

MEMORY VERSE

Even youths shall faint and be weary, and young men shall fall exhausted; but they who wait for the Lord shall renew their strength; they shall mount up with wings like eagles; they shall run and not be weary; they shall walk and not faint.
-Isaiah 40:30-31

Week Twenty-Five

I COULD DO THIS ALL DAY. [1] -STEVE ROGERS

The first time we hear this phrase, it's from a skinny, scrawny, yet very patriotic Steve Rogers as he's being pummeled by a much larger man who dared not to respect the patriotic news clips about World War II. Later, when Steve Rogers becomes Captain America, this becomes his catchphrase. He even says it to Ironman when they are fighting each other in *Captain America: Civil War.* There's even a joke about the phrase in the movie *Endgame* when an older Captain America is fighting a younger version of himself and says, *"I can do this all day,"* and the older version says, *"Yeah, I know, I know."*[2]

It's Captain America's catchphrase. Yet, every time I hear it, I think, *"This needs to be the attitude of every unbreakable man of God when he's battling sin in his life."*

It reminds me of Paul's words in Hebrews 12:1-4:

> *Therefore, since we are surrounded by so great a cloud of witnesses, let us also lay aside every weight, and sin which clings so closely, and let us run with endurance the race that is set before us,*

> *Looking to Jesus, the founder and perfecter of our faith, who for the joy that was set before him endured the cross, despising the shame, and is seated at the right hand of the throne of God.*

> *Consider him who endured from sinners such hostility against himself, so that you may not grow weary or fainthearted.*

In your struggle against sin you have not yet resisted to the point of shedding your blood. (ESV)

In these verses, Paul challenges us to do all we can to overcome sin in our lives—especially the sins that **"so easily entangle us."** (These are the ones that seem to come naturally to us and the ones we struggle the most to overcome. *The Fire Bible* says this literally refers to our most troublesome, sidetracking sins.[3])

Paul compares these sins to a *"weight"* that holds us down and keeps us from growing in our relationship with God and running the race God has for us.

The interesting thing here is that Paul doesn't say, *"If you feel like it,"* *"If you can get around to it,"* or *"Do the best you can,"* but Paul gets right to the point when he says, **"In your struggle against sin, you have not yet resisted to the point of shedding your blood."**

Can we take a moment and do a collective Joey Lawrence *"Whoa"*[4] at that last statement?

One problem that breaks too many of God's men is that we don't take our fight with sin seriously enough.

We ignore the sin in our lives and hope no one notices.

We hide it.

We make excuses and tell ourselves things like:

"It's no big deal."

"God understands."

"There's nothing I can do; everyone in my family is like this."

"I've tried to overcome before, and it didn't work; I guess it's just how it will be."

However, in his challenge in verse 4, Paul says all these excuses are bogus. They don't hold up. They aren't valid explanations at all—they are just things we say to cover up the fact that we aren't willing to fight our sins all day and gain victory. Instead, we live in our defeat and brokenness, never really becoming the men God wants us to be.

Guys, it's time for this pattern to end.

Instead of allowing the *"sins that so easily trip us up"* to dominate our lives, we need to adopt the attitude of Captain America and say, *"I can fight against this sin all day—all week—all year—for the rest of my life if necessary—but I'm never giving up, never giving in, and never letting it conquer me again. I can do this all day."*

Here's an incredible truth: Just like Steve Rogers had greater power to fight his enemies after being *"transformed"* into Captain America, you have also been transformed.

You become a new creation when you accept Jesus' offer of salvation.

> *Therefore, if anyone is in Christ, he is a new creation. The old has passed away; behold, the new has come. -2 Corinthians 5:17 (ESV)*

As a son of God, the Holy Spirit lives inside of you, empowering you.

> *The Spirit of God, who raised Jesus from the dead, lives in you. -Romans 8:11 (NLT)*

But let's go back a couple of verses in Romans 8 and see how this applies to overcoming sin:

> *But you are not controlled by your sinful nature.*
>
> *You are controlled by the Spirit if you have the Spirit of God living in you. (And remember that those who do not*

have the Spirit of Christ living in them do not belong to him at all.)

And Christ lives within you, so even though your body will die because of sin, the Spirit gives you life because you have been made right with God.

The Spirit of God, who raised Jesus from the dead, lives in you. And just as God raised Christ Jesus from the dead, he will give life to your mortal bodies by this same Spirit living within you.

Therefore, dear brothers and sisters, you have no obligation to do what your sinful nature urges you to do.
-Romans 8:9-12 (NLT)

Did you see it?

Because you are a new creature in Christ, because the Holy Spirit lives inside of you, you can fight and overcome the power of sin in your life. Because you have experienced the transforming power of salvation, you don't need to be a weak, wimpy man who is always broken by the same old sins in your life. Instead, with the help of the Holy Spirit living inside of you, you have all you need to fight and overcome any sin in your life.

When temptation comes, you can resist.

When you want to fall back into a familiar sin, you don't have to.

Instead, empowered by the Holy Spirit and armed with the sword of the Spirit, which is the Word of God, you can stand unyielding, like Captain America, and declare, *"No. I refuse to be defeated by sin. I can fight against it all day."*

SUNDAY
- [ ] Psalms 73-75

MONDAY
- [ ] 1 Samuel 21-22
- [ ] 1 Timothy 3

TUESDAY
- [ ] 1 Samuel 23-24
- [ ] 1 Timothy 4

WEDNESDAY
- [ ] 1 Samuel 25-26
- [ ] 1 Timothy 5

THURSDAY
- [ ] 1 Samuel 27-28
- [ ] 1 Timothy 6

FRIDAY
- [ ] 1 Samuel 29-31
- [ ] 2 Timothy 1

NOTES AND REFLECTION

MEMORY VERSE

This God—his way is perfect; the word of the Lord proves true; he is a shield for all those who take refuge in him. -Psalms 18:30

Week Twenty-Six

WHENEVER YOU DO SOMETHING, ACT AS IF ALL THE WORLD WERE WATCHING. - THOMAS JEFFERSON

I love these words from Thomas Jefferson! This attitude needs to be the attitude of an unbreakable man. Why?

Too many men are being broken because of sins they commit in the privacy of their own lives. They think that because no one can see them, it's okay to compromise or do things they know they shouldn't.

The dark, alone times are the most dangerous for a man of God. We will do the right thing when the eyeballs are on us, but do we stand firm when it's just us?

Secret sins are one of the biggest ways Satan traps men. He makes them think they can continue doing what they do secretly. After all, it isn't hurting anyone, and no one else knows. He encourages men to keep their sins hidden, but he doesn't tell them the whole story.

The whole story is that Satan wants you to stay bound in secret sins so that one day he can expose you! He wants to reveal what it is you are doing in secret so he can destroy you, your life, your relationship with God, and your relationship with others. He wants to shout to the world what you do in secret to humiliate you.

Satan is not the only person who wants to reveal your secret sins. God's goal is to shout your secret sins from the rooftop. How do I know this? Because the Bible says so!

For nothing is hidden that will not be made manifest, nor is anything secret that will not be known and come to light. -Luke 8:17 (ESV)

And no creature is hidden from his sight, but all are naked and exposed to the eyes of him to whom we must give account. -Hebrews 4:13 (ESV)

For God will bring every deed into judgment, with every secret thing, whether good or evil. -Ecclesiastes 12:14 (ESV)

Would not God discover this? For he knows the secrets of the heart. -Psalm 44:21 (ESV)

On that day when, according to my gospel, God judges the secrets of men by Christ Jesus. -Romans 2:16 (ESV)

Therefore whatever you have said in the dark shall be heard in the light, and what you have whispered in private rooms shall be proclaimed on the housetops. -Luke 12:3 (ESV)

You have set our iniquities before you, our secret sins in the light of your presence. -Psalms 90:8 (ESV)

"Am I only a God nearby," declares the Lord, "and not a God far away?

Who can hide in secret places so that I cannot see them?" declares the Lord. "Do not I fill heaven and earth?" declares the Lord. -Jeremiah 23:23-24 (NIV)

These verses show us that nothing is hidden from God. We may be able to hide our secret sins from others, but God sees it all! Not only does He see it all, but these verses show that He will expose our secret sin.

God wants to expose you and your secret sin because He wants to set you free.

He wants it to come to light to save you.

Satan wants to do it to destroy you. If two such powerful forces are bound and determined to expose your secret sin, how can we keep it hidden?

It is time for unbreakable men of God to stand up and say enough is enough! It is time we overcome our secret sins! How do we do it?

We do it by becoming tattletales. Remember when we were kids, there was always one kid who always told all the secrets or turned you in if he knew you did something wrong? This kid was usually labeled a tattletale. Well, it is time we become spiritual tattletales on ourselves.

Secrets lose their power when exposed to the light of truth and honesty. So, the first step to revealing our secret sin is to expose ourselves and confess the secret.

You also need to confess the sin to God and ask for forgiveness.

Why must you confess the sin if God already knows about it?

Exposing ourselves to God kills our flesh. It breaks the power the secret has over us. Exposing our secret sin frees us. So, we must confess to God and others and ask for forgiveness and deliverance from our secret sins.

Next, you have to go commando on your secret sin! You have to go to extremes with your sin. You must make restitution if your secret sin requires it (i.e., financial sins, etc).

You have to open yourself up to accountability until it hurts.

You need fellow brothers in Christ who will relentlessly hold you accountable, and you need to be honest with them about everything.

Finally, you have to commit yourself to living with honesty and integrity. All the confessing, repenting, and accountability in the world are useless if you are not committed to being free. That is why secret sin is so crippling; it is really up to you if you overcome it or not. But if you set your heart to live free of your secret sin, surrender daily to the Holy Spirit's control, and submit to the authority and accountability of others, you can be free of secret sin.

If you don't do this, your secret sin will destroy you.

That is as plain as I can say it.

The decision is yours today. Will you become an unbreakable man and conquer your secret sin? I hope your answer is a resounding YES!

SUNDAY
- [ ] Psalms 76-78

MONDAY
- [ ] 2 Samuel 1-2
- [ ] 2 Timothy 2

TUESDAY
- [ ] 2 Samuel 3-4
- [ ] 2 Timothy 3

WEDNESDAY
- [ ] 2 Samuel 5-6
- [ ] 2 Timothy 4

THURSDAY
- [ ] 2 Samuel 7-8
- [ ] Titus 1

FRIDAY
- [ ] 2 Samuel 9
- [ ] Titus 2-3

NOTES AND REFLECTION

MEMORY VERSE

Be watchful, stand firm in the faith, act like men, be strong. -1 Corinthians 16:13

Week Twenty-Seven

AND FOR THE SUPPORT OF THIS DECLARATION, WITH A FIRM RELIANCE ON THE PROTECTION OF DIVINE PROVIDENCE, WE MUTUALLY PLEDGE TO EACH OTHER OUR LIVES, OUR FORTUNES, AND OUR SACRED HONOR. -DECLARATION OF INDEPENDENCE[1]

It was the summer of 1776 in Philadelphia, Pennsylvania. Delegates from thirteen colonies gathered to *"Mutually pledge to each other their lives, fortunes, and sacred honor"[1] to support the Declaration of Independence."*

Each man knew the dangers and risks as he waited to add his signature to the document. The moment he made this pledge, he committed an act of treason against the British government.

Historically, the punishment for treason was death. Even if he wasn't captured and killed by the British government, he knew that from this day forward, he, his family, his businesses, his homes, and his fortune would be targeted for ruin by the British government.

As he stood in line waiting to sign, each man knew they weren't just sending a letter to the King of England. They were declaring war. A war they could win or lose. There was no turning back once he added his name to this document. He was putting everything on the line for the sake of freedom.

Still, fifty-six men from different colonies, backgrounds, professions, and religions signed their names to the *Declaration of Independence* on August 2, 1776.

One of the questions I often ask myself is, *"Why did they do it?"*

What drove these men to risk losing everything they held dear in their lives for a freedom they had only imagined?

Why would they risk their lives, their family's lives, and everything they had worked toward to declare war on a stronger, richer, and far more powerful government than their own?

The only answer I can find is that these men yearned for freedom more than anything else in life. They wanted it and had to have it so much that they risked everything for it. They understood the cost of freedom, and having counted it, they pledged to pay whatever price was necessary to be free.

Why did they do it? They did it because they understood something we do not---they understood what it meant to live without freedom.

When they were given the opportunity to be free, they seized the day like a starving man who craved food. With their signature, they screamed, *"Whatever it takes, I will pay the price!"*

Every freedom we enjoy is ours because fifty-six men stood in line many years ago and declared *"Independence!"* from England's King.

Sometimes, we Americans tend to take our freedom for granted. We forget that our freedom of speech, freedom of religion, and freedom to make our own choices and live our own lives came at the price of someone else's life.

As we celebrate their triumph and the inherited rewards, I ask myself, *"What can I do to follow in their footsteps?"*

Because even now, freedom is not free. The great nation we love can be lost if we don't do our part to protect it. Still, as a middle-aged man with a disability, what can I do to fight for freedom? What can we all do?

1. I can pray for my country.

Over the past year, the Holy Spirit has repeatedly reminded me of the importance of praying for our country. Worrying, watching the news, and posting on social media do very little to change the direction of our nation. But prayer is powerful.

More than anything, our country needs a revival. We need a revival where people come to know Jesus, turn from their sins, and return to Biblical principles. Not so churches can be filled, and Christians can get all the *"Pentecostal feels"* (I'm not saying that's wrong, but we need more).

If America will remain free, we need to turn back to God. If we love our country, we must intercede for its salvation and a revival that changes people's hearts and minds.

2. We must reject sin and obey God's laws.

2 Chronicles 7:14 says,

> *Then, if my people who are called by my name will humble themselves and pray and seek my face and turn from their wicked ways, I will hear from heaven and will forgive their sins and restore their land. (NLT)*

America has a massive sin problem. It isn't enough to rail against an ungodly culture and say, *"They need to change."*

Instead, we need to obey 1 Chronicles 7 and examine ourselves. As we humble ourselves and pray, we must be open to the Holy Spirit's conviction and remove any wickedness from our hearts.

Don't think your sin is as bad as what you see around you?

It doesn't matter--sin is sin. Repentance starts in the house of God.

National revival starts in our prayer closets--as we humble ourselves, repent of any sins, change, and intercede for our country.

3. We need to know what the Bible says and be willing to stand firm for truth.

When our society has rejected Biblical values, truth, and even common sense and embraced lies and sin, a person who loves their country must know what the Bible says and lovingly stand for truth.

We can't go along with lies to make people comfortable.

Truth is truth. God's ways will not change. When confronted with evil and lies, we must know what the Bible says and be willing to stand for the truth.

Will it be uncomfortable? Yes.

Will it be difficult? Uh, yeah.

But you know what else was difficult?

Freezing and going without food at Valley Forge. Writing and signing the *Declaration of Independence*, knowing their actions marked them as traitors, and if captured, they would be tortured and die.

Our founding fathers sacrificed so much so that we could be free. What are we willing to sacrifice to stay free?

In 1776, freedom had a cost. It still has a price in 2025. An unbreakable man will pay this price.

SUNDAY
- [ ] Psalms 79-81

MONDAY
- [ ] 2 Samuel 10-11
- [ ] Mark 1

TUESDAY
- [ ] 2 Samuel 12-13
- [ ] Mark 2

WEDNESDAY
- [ ] 2 Samuel 14-15
- [ ] Mark 3

THURSDAY
- [ ] 2 Samuel 16-17
- [ ] Mark 4

FRIDAY
- [ ] 2 Samuel 18-19
- [ ] Mark 5

NOTES AND REFLECTION

MEMORY VERSE

Therefore, my beloved brothers, be steadfast, immovable, always abounding in the work of the Lord, knowing that in the Lord your labor is not in vain. -1 Corinthians 15:58

Week Twenty-Eight

GIVE ME SIX HOURS TO CHOP DOWN A TREE, AND I WILL SPEND THE FIRST FOUR SHARPENING THE AXE.
-ABRAHAM LINCOLN[1]

This quote sounds like something my mentor often says to me. When I was a younger man who had just started ministry, I struggled to rest, refuel, and rejuvenate. (Truth be told, I'm still working on it.) After waiting what seemed like a long time for God to open the doors to full-time ministry, I ran through the doors and never stopped.

I loved my work and gave it everything it had. Since starting Mantour Ministries had some entrepreneurial aspects, I did what most people with a start-up do—I worked way hard for too many hours.

Then I came to the reality that many men face:

You can only chop down so many trees until the ax gets dull. Then, you must choose whether to stop and sharpen the ax or continue exhausting time and energy working with subpar equipment.

In automotive terms, you can only drive so many miles before you decide whether to stop and refuel, run out of cash, or, even worse, crash.

I finally started hearing what my mentor said when I reached this decision point.

Human beings need rest.

We need to refuel—spiritually, emotionally, mentally, and physically.

These things won't just happen. We need to work them into our schedules and choose to take time to *"sharpen our ax."*

So how do we do it?

Physically, we need rest. We can't work all the time or be stressed all the time.

We need to set boundaries that say, *"This is when I start work, and this is when I rest."* This will be challenging if you're like me, but it's necessary.

Here's another point: we must schedule this daily and longer-term.

We need to limit our daily work hours, go to bed on time, and ensure we get enough sleep.

We also need to schedule downtimes in our yearly schedule—vacations or staycations—when we say, *"I'm setting aside some time to rest and regenerate my body and mind."*

We also refuel ourselves by eating healthy foods and exercising.

We also need a little fun in our lives to help us relax.

Spiritually, we refuel by spending time in prayer and Bible reading.

If we want to stay spiritually healthy, it's essential that we have a daily quiet time with God, talk to Him, share our hearts, and enter into worship. Time in God's presence refills us and strengthens us to live as godly men.

Bible reading also refills our empty spiritual tank. Spending just a few minutes daily reading and meditating on God's Word changes our perspective. It reminds us of Who God is and who He wants us to be. It encourages us, leads us, and guides us. It isn't a *"have to"*; it's a *"get to."*

Another thing that will refill your spiritual tank is worship. Now, I'm not saying you have to grab a guitar and dance around the house singing praise and worship songs, but listening to praise and worship music will bring you into God's presence, where you can find rest and restoration.

Giving yourself a break mentally sharpens your ax. You can't work all the time. You need to have a hobby that helps you relax, refresh, and refuel. For me, this is fantasy football. It's a good outlet that gets my mind off work and allows me to interact with friends. I also enjoy listening to music.

Emotionally, it would help if you had people who would support you, encourage you, make you laugh and have fun, and refuel your tank. We can't do life alone. We must invest in the people in our lives for their sake and our own.

These are just a few things I'm learning in my life. Slowly, I am learning what old Abe said is true. We are not meant to run on empty. It just isn't possible—without refueling, we will eventually break.

If we want to be unbreakable men, we must examine our lives and ask, *"Where do I need to sharpen my ax?"* Then, we need to make a plan to start doing it.

> **Come to me, all who labor and are heavy laden, and I will give you rest. -Matthew 11:28 (ESV)**

SUNDAY
- [ ] Psalms 82-84

MONDAY
- [ ] 2 Samuel 20-21
- [ ] Mark 6

TUESDAY
- [ ] 2 Samuel 22-23
- [ ] Mark 7

WEDNESDAY
- [ ] 2 Samuel 24
- [ ] Mark 8-9

THURSDAY
- [ ] Habakkuk 1-2
- [ ] Mark 10

FRIDAY
- [ ] Habakkuk 3
- [ ] Mark 11-12

NOTES AND REFLECTION

MEMORY VERSE

Let us not grow weary of doing good, for in due season we will reap, if we do not give up.
-Galatians 6:9

Week Twenty-Nine

I DO BELIEVE; HELP ME OVERCOME MY UNBELIEF!
-MARK 9:24

These are some of my favorite words in the Bible. They are so honest and raw. Where do we read them?

Mark 9 shares this verse with us. It is spoken moments after Jesus had been transfigured on the mountain. He, along with Peter, James, and John, returned to the rest of the disciples, only to find them in a fight with the teachers of the law. Talk about being brought back into reality.

Jesus asked His disciples what all the commotion was about. He was answered by someone in the crowd who explained that he had brought his son, who was possessed by a demon that beat and tortured the boy. The boy's father asked the disciples to cast the demon out, but they couldn't do it.

What a tragic situation. This man had to watch his son be attacked, overcome, and mutilated by this demon. It is obvious that this has been going on for some time. He had to watch his son suffer, and he had no way to help him.

Now, he came to Jesus for help. However, Jesus was gone when he came to the disciples, and although the disciples were doing their best, they could do little to help.

The demon in the boy hated being around Jesus.

Jesus asked the boy's father, "How long has he been like this?"

"From childhood," he answered. "It has often thrown him into fire or water to kill him. But if you can do anything, take pity on us and help us." -Mark 9:21-22 (NIV)

This man's heart is breaking. He can't take anymore. As many of us do, he cried out to Jesus for help. However, he asks for help in a questioning way. This fact didn't go unnoticed by Jesus.

"If you can?" said Jesus. "Everything is possible for one who believes." -Mark 9:23 (NIV)

These words touched the man deeply, and he uttered what I believe is the best and most honest prayer in the Bible.

Immediately the boy's father exclaimed, "I do believe; help me overcome my unbelief!" -Mark 9:24 (NIV)

What an honest statement! Anyone who has ever gone through a hard time can relate to this man's statement. He **knows** Jesus has the power to set his son free. Yet disappointment and the pain of our experiences make us wonder **IF** God will help us.

This man believed, yet he was tired and emotionally drained. In this state of mind, he wondered if Jesus would help him.

So, he confessed his faith and asked Jesus to give him the hope and strength to continue believing.

Notice Jesus didn't rebuke the man for his statement but instead showed compassion and strengthened his faith. The man's prayer showed he fully relied on Jesus to give him the strength to continue believing.

Despite the man's struggle with unbelief, Jesus acknowledged his faith and healed his son. As a result, he saw his son miraculously delivered and set free.

This man is a model for how we should handle our times of difficulty. I often find myself praying this prayer. There are many times when I struggle to believe that God will help me. I know that God has the ability and power to assist me, but when I am exhausted and beaten down by life's pain and hardships, my faith wavers. I start to think that God won't help me and that I'll be stuck in my situation forever.

During these times, I recall this powerful prayer and cry out to God, saying, *"I believe You can help me. I believe You have the power to set me free from this trial. I believe Your power can get me through this. However, I find it hard to believe that You will help me. I struggle with the thought that You might let me down. I doubt that You will come through for me. Father, I believe, but please help my unbelief!"*

I often find that God strengthens my faith in various ways. I might hear an inspiring song, read a comforting verse in the Bible, or receive encouragement from someone. God always finds a way to help my unbelief.

I am thankful Mark was inspired to include this prayer in the Bible. It is truly a unique and honest prayer and an excellent model of praying during challenging times.

What about you?

Do you have a relationship that makes your faith waver?

Do you deal with a physical infirmity that sometimes wears you down and makes you think God isn't going to help you through?

Are you a parent wrestling in the Heavenlies for the soul of your child, scared they won't turn back to God?

Are you struggling financially and are fearful that God won't keep His Word to supply your needs?

Have you lost your job and struggled to believe God will supply a new job for you?

Do you ever think, *"God will never help me?"*

Does your situation seem hopeless?

Do you feel God is unable to set you free?

Are you feeling overwhelmed?

Has the pain and heartache of your situation left you struggling for help?

I understand the hardships and exhaustion this brings. I encourage you to pray the prayer that this father prayed.

Tell God you believe He has the power to help you, but the burden you carry causes you to doubt that He WILL help you. Ask Him for hope and encouragement to continue.

I am sure this is a prayer God will answer. He did it for this father, and He has done it for me. He will do it for you, too.

SUNDAY
☐ Psalms 85-87

MONDAY
☐ Daniel 1-2

☐ Mark 13-14

TUESDAY
☐ Daniel 3-4

☐ Mark 15-16

WEDNESDAY
☐ Daniel 5-6

☐ Hebrews 1

THURSDAY
☐ Hosea 1-2

☐ Hebrews 2

FRIDAY
☐ Hosea 3-4

☐ Hebrews 3

NOTES AND REFLECTION

MEMORY VERSE

For though we walk in the flesh, we are not waging war according to the flesh. For the weapons of our warfare are not of the flesh but have divine power to destroy strongholds. -2 Corinthians 10:3-4

Week Thirty

OUR ACUTE NEED IS TO CULTIVATE A WILLINGNESS TO LEARN AND TO REMAIN TEACHABLE.[1] -CHUCK SWINDOLL

I was so angry. Sitting across the table and listening, I could not believe what I heard.

How could he say those things about me?

I completely disagreed with his perspective.

I was totally blind to the obvious flaw in my life and was shocked by his correction.

The funny thing is that in the next two months, I realized he was absolutely 100% completely right. I was so glad that I had decided to follow my lifelong commitment to maintain a teachable attitude, keep my mouth shut, and follow the advice of godly mentors. Because even though I didn't see it immediately, it was excellent advice.

I have learned this throughout my life: being an unbreakable man means being a teachable man who can take correction and criticism from mature, godly leaders.

I've also seen a lack of teachableness break too many.

I've seen the story so many times that it hardly surprises me anymore. A man receives criticism, rebuke, or correction and absolutely cannot take it. He can't see what his mentor or coach is trying to teach him. Instead, he gets offended. His feelings get hurt. His ego is wounded. Sure that his mentor is wrong, he storms out the door, licking his wounds. Over the following days, weeks, and months, he tells everyone who will listen about how cruelly and unfairly he was treated by one who was trying to help him.

The sad thing is that this scenario often ends the same way: seeing only the offense and never searching for the truth, the man continues as he is. Years later, he is broken by the very thing he was warned about earlier.

Like the man who insisted that the *"Do Not Enter, Flooding Ahead"* sign didn't apply to him, he continued on and fell into danger.

It's heartbreaking every time.

That's why it's essential that you learn to accept correction if you want to be an unbreakable man of God. Because here's the truth: we all have areas that need improvement. Often, others can see these things way before we do.

When a trustworthy person points these things out and tries to help us, the best thing we can do is heed the warning. At the very least, we should spend significant time in prayer, asking the Holy Spirit to show us if the correction is legitimate. That's what I did with the story in the beginning, and yep, the Holy Spirit helped me see that the rebuke was real and I needed to make a change.

Here's a fact about correction: When a godly person gives advice, criticism, or correction, it will strengthen you.

Listening to their advice and making the changes they see as necessary will make you unbreakable.

However, if you ignore their advice, your arrogance will ultimately break you. That's why the Bible provides so many Scriptures on the benefits of being teachable and taking advice. Here are a few:

Whoever loves discipline loves knowledge, but whoever hates correction is stupid. -Proverbs 12:1 (NIV)

The wise in heart accept commands, but a chattering fool comes to ruin. -Proverbs 10:8 (NIV)

The way of fools seems right to them, but the wise listen to advice. -Proverbs 12:15 (NIV)

Where there is strife, there is pride, but wisdom is found in those who take advice. -Proverbs 13:10 (NIV)

In the same way, you who are younger, submit yourselves to your elders. All of you, clothe yourselves with humility toward one another, because, "God opposes the proud but shows favor to the humble. -1 Peter 5:5 (NIV)

If we want to be unbreakable men of God, one of the best things we can do is learn to take advice.

SUNDAY
- [ ] Psalms 88-90

MONDAY
- [ ] Hosea 5-6
- [ ] Hebrews 4

TUESDAY
- [ ] Hosea 7-8
- [ ] Hebrews 5

WEDNESDAY
- [ ] Hosea 9-10
- [ ] Hebrews 6

THURSDAY
- [ ] Hosea 11-12
- [ ] Hebrews 7

FRIDAY
- [ ] Hosea 13-14
- [ ] Hebrews 8

NOTES AND REFLECTION

MEMORY VERSE

This God—his way is perfect; the word of the Lord proves true; he is a shield for all those who take refuge in him. -Psalms 18:30

Week Thirty-One

AND I KNOW WHAT I HAVE TO DO NOW. I GOTTA KEEP BREATHING. BECAUSE TOMORROW THE SUN WILL RISE. WHO KNOWS WHAT THE TIDE COULD BRING?[1]
-CHUCK NOLAND

This quote comes from Tom Hanks' film *Castaway*. For those of you who've never seen the movie, Hanks plays Chuck Noland, a FedEx employee stranded on a deserted island after a plane crash that killed everyone else on board. After surviving at least four years on the island, Chuck manages to build a raft that takes him to the sea, where he is rescued by a passing ship.

Then comes my favorite part of the movie: When he returns to civilization, Chuck faces a new reality, starting with the fact that everyone gave him up for dead years ago. They had a funeral, and legally, he was dead.

Not only had his friends assumed he was dead, but his fiancé had moved on. She was now married with a young daughter. In the over four years that he was gone, everything had changed.

That's where we find this quote. Tom Hanks's character pours out his heart to his friend, whose wife had passed away while he was on the island, telling him about the time on the island when he knew he had absolutely no control over his life or the situation.

"And that's when this feeling came over me like a warm blanket. I knew, somehow, that I had to stay alive.

Somehow. I had to keep breathing. Even though there was no reason to hope. And all my logic said that I would never see this place again. So that's what I did. I stayed alive. I kept breathing. And one day my logic was proven all wrong because the tide came in, and gave me a sail.

And now, here I am. I'm back. In Memphis, talking to you. I have ice in my glass... And I've lost her all over again. I'm so sad that I don't have Kelly. But I'm so grateful that she was with me on that island.

And I know what I have to do now. I gotta keep breathing. Because tomorrow the sun will rise. Who knows what the tide could bring?"[1]

Here's the thing: hopefully, very few of us will ever be stranded on a desert island. However, we all go through times in life that we never planned, never expected, and quite honestly hoped would never happen.

- When we're fighting the disease

- When we lost the job we loved and are struggling financially

- When the person who meant the most to us in the world passes away

- When we are in a genuinely bad place and have no idea how to escape, change the circumstances, or even make time pass more quickly

What do we do when we realize we can't control anything about our situation, and we feel as alone and hopeless as the man who was a castaway on a desert island?

We keep breathing.

We keep moving forward.

We get up in the morning, pray, read the Bible, and keep doing what we need to do.

We keep hoping.

We keep believing what the Bible says is true and that someday, God will work everything out for His purpose for those who love Him.

> ***And we know that God causes everything to work together for the good of those who love God and are called according to his purpose for them. -Romans 8:28 (NLT)***

Most importantly, we realize that unlike Tom Hanks's character, who only had a volleyball to keep him company, you are never alone as a child of God.

Jesus promises that He will never leave us or forsake us. (Hebrews 13:5, Deuteronomy 31:8)

In good times and especially in hard times, He is walking right beside us, helping us, strengthening us, and, when necessary, carrying us.

As sons of God, we can be sure that even when we can't control our circumstances, God is in control.

He has a plan. He has a purpose. He knows what is happening, and He will get us through.

Trusting in the Bible's truths and God's promises, we keep breathing in and out every day. Keep moving forward and waiting for God to send the tide that changes everything.

That's how you remain unbreakable in the most desperate circumstances.

SUNDAY
- [ ] **Psalms 91-93**

MONDAY
- [ ] **Joel 1**
- [ ] **Hebrews 9**

TUESDAY
- [ ] **Joel 2-3**
- [ ] **Hebrews 10**

WEDNESDAY
- [ ] **Obadiah 1**
- [ ] **Hebrews 11**

THURSDAY
- [ ] **1 Kings 1-2**
- [ ] **Hebrews 12**

FRIDAY
- [ ] **1 Kings 3, 4:20-34**
- [ ] **Hebrews 13**

NOTES AND REFLECTION

MEMORY VERSE

So we do not lose heart. Though our outer self is wasting away, our inner self is being renewed day by day. -2 Corinthians 4:16

Week Thirty-Two

EVEN IF HE DOESN'T, WE WILL NOT BOW!
-SHADRACH, MESHACH, AND ABEDNEGO

A while back, I spent the day with some friends who have little kids. We played all kinds of games, including a rousing round of *"Simon Says."* (I have to admit, this was the first time I played this game in years.)

Watching the little ones do the nutty things that I would tell them to do was funny.

Simon says, *"Scratch your tummy."*

Simon says, *"Do a somersault."*

Simon says, *"Jump around like a little monkey."*

It was a fun ten minutes (until they got bored and moved on). Later, I began to wonder, *"Do you ever feel like you're playing a game of Simon Says in today's culture?"*

Simon says, *"Don't say that."*

Simon says, *"You can't think this."*

Simon says, *"You have to believe what I believe."*

It's one of the most significant challenges Christians face today: Choosing whether or not they will play along or refuse to bow to the voices of a secular, anti-Christian society.

It's just like the situation found in Daniel 3, where three followers of God had to choose to bow or not to bow.

In this passage, we meet Shadrach, Meschach, and Abednego. They had been taken into captivity in Babylon and put through serious training. Now, their season of training has passed, and they are now described as *"Jews whom you have set over the affairs of the province of Babylon." (Daniel 3:12, NIV)*

Although their positions have changed, their challenges have not. Instead, they've grown even more difficult. As we read through Daniel 3, we see that these men must choose to obey God at the risk of their lives.

The story is pretty simple: King Nebuchadnezzar gets the ridiculous idea that he wants the world to bow down and worship him. So he builds a gigantic statue and declares that everyone must come, bow down, and worship his statue whenever the music plays. Those who didn't bow were destined to die.

Once again, Shadrach, Meshach, and Abednego face a choice. Obeying the king's order meant disobeying God's Law.

Shadrach, Meshach, and Abednego decided to obey God rather than man.

They did not bow.

Even when a group of snitches went to the king and said, *"These men won't bow"*....(Daniel 3:12)

Even when the king said, *"Bow or I'll throw you into the fiery furnace"*.... (Daniel 3:14-15)

Even when they made the furnace ten times hotter—so hot that even the men who were escorting them to the furnace died from the heat. (Daniel 3:19-22)

Shadrach, Meshach, and Abednego said, *"We won't bow."*

Specifically, they said:

If we are thrown into the blazing furnace, the God we serve is able to deliver us from it, and he will deliver us from Your Majesty's hand. But even if he does not, we want you to know, Your Majesty, that we will not serve your gods or worship the image of gold you have set up.
-Daniel 3:17-18 (NIV)

"But even if he does not"....

What a powerful statement!

Whether God does a miracle or they suffer consequences for our stand for Christ, we will still follow Him.

Today, they stand as an example to all of us who are faced with the temptation to bow to a society that has replaced truth with tolerance and increasingly demands that we compromise our beliefs to make others more comfortable.

In a world that says, *"All roads lead to Heaven, you can't say that there is only one God and one road to salvation."*

To all who say, *"The Bible is old-fashioned...it can't be taken literally...it doesn't apply to today."*

To all who try to quiet the voice of truth and silence the Church, we need to follow the example of Shadrach, Meshach, and Abednego and say, **"We won't bow."**

Here's what's even more impressive about these three men: they said they wouldn't bow, **NO MATTER WHAT.**

They trusted that God would come through for them, yet they said, *"EVEN IF HE DOESN'T,"* we still won't bow.

The truth is that sometimes, refusing to bow comes at a cost.

For some, refusing to compromise Biblical truth could cost them friends and family members.

Others may lose income, jobs, and invitations to events or clubs.

Eventually, some may be called to prison or even die for Jesus.

Today is the day to make your choice, to determine in your heart, and to pray that whatever situation arises, you will have the courage and conviction of Shadrach, Meshach, and Abednego. Pray for unbreakable courage and strength to stand firm no matter what the culture demands. Let's be the ones in the crowd who will not bow. Follow the example of Shadrach, Meshach, and Abednego and live by the words that say, ***"No matter what, I will not bow."***

SUNDAY
☐ Psalms 94-96

MONDAY
☐ 1 Kings 5, 6:11-14

☐ 1 Corinthians 1

TUESDAY
☐ 1 Kings 8-9

☐ 1 Corinthians 2

WEDNESDAY
☐ 1 Kings 10-11

☐ 1 Corinthians 3

THURSDAY
☐ 1 Kings 12-13

☐ 1 Corinthians 4

FRIDAY
☐ 1 Kings 14-15

☐ 1 Corinthians 5

NOTES AND REFLECTION

MEMORY VERSE

Persecuted, but not forsaken; struck down, but not destroyed. -2 Corinthians 4:9

Week Thirty-Three

ALWAYS STAND ON PRINCIPLE...EVEN IF YOU STAND ALONE.
-JOHN ADAMS[1]

The older I get, the more I believe in the importance of having strong personal convictions—unshakeable beliefs that you are willing to fight for, die for, or, more commonly, stand firm on.

As Christians living in the twenty-first century, these convictions are frequently attacked. Still, we cannot compromise in these areas. Instead, we must stand firm.

Throughout my life, I have always believed I was a man of strong convictions. I've always been passionate about what I believed in and have done my best to stand by those convictions, no matter what. And yet, it wasn't until I reached my late thirties or early forties that I truly saw the importance of identifying my convictions. By that, I mean taking time to sit down and list beliefs and convictions I was unwilling to bend. As always, this decision resulted from hard times when people asked me to bend, and I realized I just could not.

I want Paul's words to be able to be said to me.

> *Only let your manner of life be worthy of the gospel of Christ, so that whether I come and see you or am absent, I may hear of you that you are standing firm in one spirit, with one mind striving side by side for the faith of the gospel. -Philippians 1:27 (ESV)*

Sure, it is often easier to bend or compromise, but at the end of the day, I have to look in the mirror and respect what I see. I'm the one who is going before God in prayer, knowing that I put pleasing someone else over pleasing Him. Ultimately, I'm the one who will have to give account to God for my life. This includes every decision, every word, and every compromise. (Matthew 12:36-37) When that day comes, I want to hear Him say, *"Well done,"* not *"What were you thinking?"*

This is why we all need to be men of conviction. It means identifying what we believe and how far we will go to stand by those beliefs.

One thing that helped me through this process was making a list of beliefs that I could not compromise. This list included essential beliefs and personal convictions that I could not abandon.

It's important not to minimize the value of personal convictions, even if they seem insignificant in the grand scheme of things. Over the years, I have learned that how we respond when our personal convictions are questioned helps us prepare for the times when our concrete beliefs are attacked.

This is the heart of an unbreakable man of God. He knows what he believes and refuses to abandon his convictions.

SUNDAY
☐ **Psalms 97-100**

MONDAY
☐ **1 Kings 16-17**

☐ **1 Corinthians 6**

TUESDAY
☐ **1 Kings 18-19**

☐ **1 Corinthians 7**

WEDNESDAY
☐ **1 Kings 20-21**

☐ **1 Corinthians 8**

THURSDAY
☐ **1 Kings 22**

☐ **1 Corinthians 9**

FRIDAY
☐ **2 Kings 1-2**

☐ **1 Corinthians 10**

NOTES AND REFLECTION

MEMORY VERSE

Cast your burden on the Lord, and he will sustain you; he will never permit the righteous to be moved. -Psalms 55:22

Week Thirty-Four

LORD, DO NOT HOLD THIS SIN AGAINST THEM. -STEPHEN

Forgiveness. It's always challenging.

Especially when you're being stoned to death just for preaching the Gospel like Stephen. And yet, as we look at Acts 7, we see that these were Stephen's final words in this situation.

> *Now when they heard these things they were enraged, and they ground their teeth at him.*
>
> *But he, full of the Holy Spirit, gazed into heaven and saw the glory of God, and Jesus standing at the right hand of God.*
>
> *And he said, "Behold, I see the heavens opened, and the Son of Man standing at the right hand of God." But they cried out with a loud voice and stopped their ears and rushed together at him.*
>
> *Then they cast him out of the city and stoned him. And the witnesses laid down their garments at the feet of a young man named Saul.*
>
> *And as they were stoning Stephen, he called out, "Lord Jesus, receive my spirit."*
>
> *And falling to his knees he cried out with a loud voice, "Lord, do not hold this sin against them."*
>
> *And when he had said this, he fell asleep. -Acts 7:54-60 (ESV)*

In these verses, Stephen sets the example for forgiveness, which makes us unbreakable men of God. Unforgiveness breaks us, but when we forgive, the pain meant to destroy us loses its power over us, making us unbreakable.

But Jamie, you don't know what happened to me. I can't forgive.

Perhaps that's because you don't completely understand forgiveness. Here are some facts about forgiveness that might help.

1. Forgiveness heals you.

Imagine someone dumping garbage all over you. It wasn't your fault; they had no right to do it. However, now the choice rests with you—will you live covered in the garbage or shake off the trash, take a bath, and move on?

Straight truth: Forgiveness is how you shake off the garbage.

2. Forgiveness is not condoning the other person's behavior as acceptable or no big deal.

It isn't a get-out-of-jail-free card for people who aren't really sorry and don't want to change their lives.

When we realize that forgiveness isn't saying, *"Oh, it's okay that you did this, or it's no big deal,"* we can put things into perspective and forgive.

3. Forgiveness doesn't mean you have to forget.

Realistically, you can't forget what happened. It's part of your story. Forgiveness will heal your heart and take away the pain when you remember. That's how I can write about my past or tell my story in a sermon. It doesn't hurt anymore. I can't forget the facts, but I no longer have to live trapped in the pain.

4. Forgiveness doesn't mean you don't bring it up again.

Talking about issues is the key to freedom. Talking is healthy. Suppressing hurts, and keeping secrets is unhealthy. God wants us to be healthy.

5. Forgiveness doesn't mean you have to put your heart on the line to be hurt by someone who is unrepentant and unchanged.

Just because God commands us to forgive does not mean that He wants us to allow people to abuse us, demean us, or diminish our dignity without establishing boundaries. That would be unwise. God wants His children to be wise.

Healthy boundaries are choices that you make to proceed in a safer, healthier, and more beneficial manner to live a peaceful life.

6. Forgiveness is not about the other person.

Forgiveness is a gift you give yourself. It's how you let the other person to God and move on with your life. It's how you go of the pain and free yourself to be an unbreakable man of God.

As I said before, unforgiveness breaks us. However, when we forgive, the pain meant to destroy us loses its power over us, making us unbreakable.

Stephen did it.

Jesus did it.

You can do it, too.

SUNDAY
- [ ] Psalms 101-104

MONDAY
- [ ] 2 Kings 3-4
- [ ] 1 Corinthians 11

TUESDAY
- [ ] 2 Kings 5-6
- [ ] 1 Corinthians 12

WEDNESDAY
- [ ] 2 Kings 7-8
- [ ] 1 Corinthians 13

THURSDAY
- [ ] 2 Kings 9-10
- [ ] 1 Corinthians 14

FRIDAY
- [ ] 2 Kings 11-12
- [ ] 1 Corinthians 15

NOTES AND REFLECTION

MEMORY VERSE

He restores my soul. He leads me in paths of righteousness for his name's sake. -Psalms 23:3

Week Thirty-Five

GOD DOES NOT REQUIRE THAT YOU BE SUCCESSFUL; ONLY THAT YOU BE FAITHFUL. -MOTHER TERESA[1]

As men, we naturally tend to base our worth on what we do, our careers, and what we accomplish. But this quote reminds us that our success as unbreakable men stems from being faithful to God. Our value in God's eyes is not measured by our achievements but by our unwavering commitment to Him.

Faithfulness is not about the greatness of our accomplishments or the recognition we receive from others. It is about the quiet, consistent dedication to doing what is right, even when no one is watching. It is about trusting God with the outcome, knowing His plans are far greater than ours.

God calls us to be faithful in the small things, our everyday choices, our relationships, our spiritual disciplines, and our responsibilities.

> *Moreover, it is required of stewards that they be found faithful. -1 Corinthians 4:2 (ESV)*

Being faithful means persevering through challenges, remaining steadfast in our beliefs, and serving others with love and humility. It means showing up, day after day, even when the path is difficult or success seems out of reach. This consistent commitment is what makes us unbreakable men.

God sees what the world deems success, but it isn't His definition of success. He instead looks at our hearts, our intentions, and faithfulness. When we trust Him, we are freed from the pressure to bend to the world's definition of success and can focus instead on living a life that pleases Him.

An unbreakable man uses his strength to remain faithful every day. He continues to trust in God's plan for his life and finds peace in knowing that our worth is not defined by our successes but by our commitment to walking in faith. Let's remember this reminder from Mother Teresa that it is not the results that matter most but the faithfulness with which we live our lives.

SUNDAY
☐ **Psalms 105-108**

MONDAY
☐ **2 Kings 13-14**

☐ **1 Corinthians 16**

TUESDAY
☐ **2 Kings 15-16**

☐ **James 1**

WEDNESDAY
☐ **2 Kings 17-18**

☐ **James 2**

THURSDAY
☐ **2 Kings 19-20**

☐ **James 3**

FRIDAY
☐ **2 Kings 21-22**

☐ **James 4**

NOTES AND REFLECTION

MEMORY VERSE

Do you not know that in a race all the runners run, but only one receives the prize? So run that you may obtain it. -1 Corinthians 9:24

Week Thirty-Six

DON'T EXPECT TO BE MOTIVATED EVERY DAY TO GET OUT THERE AND MAKE THINGS HAPPEN. YOU WON'T BE. DON'T COUNT ON MOTIVATION. COUNT ON DISCIPLINE.[1]
-JOCKO WILLINK

Daniel just received a big promotion. When I say *"big promotion,"* I mean he just stepped into a super, ginormous job of a lifetime.

When King Darius conquered King Belshazzar (after the infamous *"writing on the wall"* in Daniel 5), he set up a new government structure. He gave 120 men the job of *"satrap"* (governors), then he appointed 3 of them as *"vice-regents"* (head of the governor). Daniel was one of the *"vice-regents"* until he got the promotion that put him in charge of the whole kingdom. Yep, you read that right——the WHOLE kingdom. (Daniel 6:1-3)

Needless to say, this made the other governors jealous. Who was this Daniel guy that he got such a huge position——to even rule over them—men who probably had more training and experience than Daniel, a former Jewish exile?

In a sentence, the powers that be were livid. They started designing a plot to take Daniel down.

There was only one problem——they couldn't find any dirt on Daniel to make him look bad. His character was impeccable.

The Message says this:

> *The vice-regents and governors got together to find some old scandal or skeleton in Daniel's life that they could use*

against him, but they couldn't dig up anything. He was totally exemplary and trustworthy. They could find no evidence of negligence or misconduct. -Daniel 6:4, (MSG)

What an incredible reputation!! What an example for all of us to strive toward! They couldn't find anything to use against him because he was exemplary and trustworthy. Wow!!

Then it hit them: If they wanted to trap Daniel, they had to make him do what he would never do—disobey God's Law.

And so, in Daniel 6:6-9, we see the conspirators go to the king and get him to make a law saying that no one could pray to anyone but the king for thirty days. If they did, they would be thrown into the den of lions.

I have to admit, having been raised in the church, I have heard the story of Daniel and the lion's den hundreds of times. I've seen pictures of lions on felt boards, watched the *VeggieTales* videos, and heard countless sermons. But it was only recently, as I reread this chapter, that I noticed a few little words hidden in Daniel 6:10.

But when Daniel learned that the law had been signed, he went home and knelt down as usual in his upstairs room, with its windows open toward Jerusalem. He prayed three times a day, just as he had always done, giving thanks to his God. (NLT)

Daniel did exactly what they expected him to do. (Daniel 6:10)

"Just as he always did," Daniel remained faithful to God's Law.

Just as he did when he was a young man who refused to eat the king's food.

Just like he wasn't at the king's party worshiping idols and desecrating the Temple objects the night the kingdom fell.

Once again, Daniel said, *"No matter the cost, I will cling to God's Laws. I will be faithful to God. Obedience is my highest priority. Whatever happens, I will not sin against God."*

That's an unbreakable man of God!

But what gave Daniel the strength to hold to his commitment?

I believe part of the answer is that prayer and spending time with God were normal parts of his life. In fact, by this point, spending time with God, seeking God's wisdom, and hearing God give His wisdom had become an integral part of Daniel's life.

Because he did it every day, he knew he couldn't survive without it.

He knew his time with God gave him everything he needed to lead the country and fulfill his responsibilities.

He knew his commitment to God had brought him to this point, and he would not give up this time for anyone or anything.

For Daniel, prayer wasn't a *"have-to."* It was an *"I get to"* and *"I need to."*

Because he had developed the discipline of prayer, he knew he could not survive without it. He depended on it. It was more precious to him than life, so he chose prayer...just like always.

Here's the thing: if we want to be unbreakable like Daniel in the hard times, we need to discipline ourselves to develop consistency in our prayer life and Bible reading before the difficulty comes.

This isn't going to just magically happen.

You'll have to create a plan to pray and then do everything you can to stick to that plan.

First, you need to choose a time when prayer works for you. Look at your schedule and say, *"This is when I can realistically pray,"* then put it on your calendar like an appointment.

Next, choose a place to pray. Choose one place where you can spend time alone, uninterrupted. Let the people who live with you know when you are there, and the door is closed, you are praying.

Finally, stick to the plan—even when you don't feel like it.

Jocko Willink says, *"Don't expect to be motivated every day to get out there and make things happen. You won't be. Don't count on motivation. Count on Discipline."*[1]

Daniel didn't start praying when the people who hated him passed the law. Instead, he could stand firm for God and His principles because he had the foundation of a personal relationship with God.

Today, if you want to follow Daniel's example and be an unbreakable man, you must discipline yourself to start spending time in your prayer closet.

Be faithful, consistent, and committed to developing a personal relationship with Jesus.

That's how you prepare for the day when the command comes to bow. You can say, ***"Just like I've always done, I only bow my knee to Jesus."***

SUNDAY
- [ ] Psalms 109-112

MONDAY
- [ ] 2 Kings 23-24
- [ ] James 5

TUESDAY
- [ ] 2 Kings 25
- [ ] 1 Peter 1

WEDNESDAY
- [ ] Ecclesiastes 1-2
- [ ] 1 Peter 2

THURSDAY
- [ ] Ecclesiastes 3-4
- [ ] 1 Peter 3

FRIDAY
- [ ] Ecclesiastes 5-6
- [ ] 1 Peter 4

NOTES AND REFLECTION

MEMORY VERSE

Every athlete exercises self-control in all things. They do it to receive a perishable wreath, but we an imperishable.
-1 Corinthians 9:25

Week Thirty-Seven

"LET'S ROLL" [1] -TODD BEAMER

Most of us remember where we were when the plane hit the first tower. I'd just switched on the television to hear the recap of *Monday Night Football* when horror struck.

First, one plane, then two. Next, a plane hit the Pentagon.

The world watched as people were trapped inside the burning buildings. No one knew what would happen next. All flights were suspended from taking off, but there were still flights in the air. Would there be more attacks? What would happen next?

What most of us did not know at the time was that there was another hijacked plane in the air filled with passengers. Because their plane took off late, the passengers on Flight 93 knew the fate of the other hijacked planes and decided that together, they would fight back and take control of the aircraft.

The words *"Let's Roll"* were the final words of Todd Beamer.

They were the words of an unbreakable man who represented the unbreakable spirit of all those on the plane as they attempted to take control of the plane and stop a fourth attack.

While they successfully saved the lives of those who would have been the target of the fourth attack, they lost their own in the process. They died heroes. Men and women who knew the truth of John 15:13, ***"Greater love has no one than this, that someone lay down his life for his friends." (ESV)***

This spirit lived inside the unbreakable men and women who ran toward the buildings that day. Firefights, police officers, EMS, and emergency workers witnessed the horror of the tragedy and ran to do all they could to help save a life.

This same spirit came alive in the many men and women who joined the armed services to respond to that horrible day. They joined to serve, to fight and defend the nation they loved, and if necessary, to lay down their lives.

This week, we will honor those who demonstrated unbreakable courage in the face of unthinkable hate and tragedy.

We vow that we will never forget.

We will honor them, and we will honor their families.

We will also choose to honor their sacrifice by following President Barack Obama's words: *"Even the smallest act of service, the simplest act of kindness, is a way to honor those we lost, a way to reclaim that spirit of unity that followed 9/11."*[2]

Each day, we honor the unbreakable sacrifice of those who gave so much when we answer our call to serve, sacrifice, be kind, help a neighbor, or show the love of Christ. When your community, neighbor, church, or family needs you, will you answer as Todd Beamer did and say, *"Yes. I'm there. Let's roll?"*

Will you follow the example of those who serve when it's challenging and sacrifice until it hurts? Can those around you depend on you to be unbreakable?

SUNDAY
- [ ] Psalms 113-115

MONDAY
- [ ] Ecclesiastes 7-8
- [ ] 1 Peter 5

TUESDAY
- [ ] Ecclesiastes 9-10
- [ ] 2 Peter 1

WEDNESDAY
- [ ] Ecclesiastes 11
- [ ] 2 Peter 2

THURSDAY
- [ ] Ecclesiastes 12
- [ ] 2 Peter 3

FRIDAY
- [ ] Jeremiah 1-3
- [ ] 2 Corinthians 1

NOTES AND REFLECTION

MEMORY VERSE

So I do not run aimlessly; I do not box as one beating the air. -1 Corinthians 9:26

Week Thirty-Eight

AND WHO KNOWS WHETHER YOU HAVE NOT COME TO THE KINGDOM FOR SUCH A TIME AS THIS? -MORDECAI

Here's an interesting fact about this quote: when most of us hear it, our minds immediately go to Queen Esther. It's often considered a *"women's quote"* and used at many Women's Conferences.

But here's the thing—this quote was actually said by a MAN—Mordecai. They are the words of a godly man encouraging a woman in his family to step into her God-given calling and responsibility.

For those not familiar with the story of Mordecai and Esther, let's recap. Mordecai was a Jew living as an exile in Persia. Esther 2 tells us that his father was one of the captives taken away from Jerusalem by Nebuchadnezzar. Mordecai was born and raised in captivity, but he is still fiercely loyal to his Jewish faith. Other than that dedication, nothing seems to be exceptional about him. He's just a godly man living his life.

Until there's a tragedy in his family. At some point, his uncle died and left behind an orphan daughter, Esther. Being a good man, Mordecai took her into his home and raised her as his own.

As we read the book of Esther, we see that when she was grown, though a series of events, Esther was chosen to the the queen of the land. Yet, Mordecai didn't abandon her. He continued to watch over her, advise her, and support her in her new role.

Then came the day that Mordecai heard the horrific news. Thanks to the evil Haman, a date was set for all Jews throughout the kingdom of Ahasuerus to be destroyed. Mordecai's first reaction was to put on sackcloth and ashes and cry out in a loud voice.

Then he remembered...Esther. This must be why God allowed her to become the Queen.

So he goes to Esther and tells her about the decree. He then makes his plea—you need to help your people. After Esther says, *"I can't do that,"* Mordecai says his famous words.

And who knows whether you have not come to the kingdom for such a time as this? -Esther 4:14 (ESV)

But he doesn't stop there—after Esther accepts his challenge to go to the king, Mordecai organizes all the Jews to fast and pray for Esther.

Later, when God answers their prayer and turns the king's heart, Mordecai is seen once again advising Esther and working alongside her to save their people.

Now, you may be asking, *"Great story. But what does all of this have to do with being an unbreakable man of God?"*

Here it is: All too often, broken men who needed healing from the hurts and wounds in their own lives have tried to take Scripture out of context to suppress, subdue, and stifle the women in their lives. Rather than learning the truth that a proper reading of the Bible shows that Judea-Christian values have been the historical leaders in promoting dignity and value in women, these men have allowed broken egos and insecurities to keep women from walking into their God-given responsibilities, destinies, and callings.

This is not God's will, and it is not Biblical.

As we read in the Gospels, Jesus sets the example of treating women with dignity and respect, encouraging them to hear His teaching, and allowing them to play a role in His ministry. He even honored a woman by allowing her to be the first to see His resurrected body and tell the good news of what she saw.

Yet even before Jesus, we have Biblical examples of godly men encouraging women to be who God called them to be and do what God called them to do. Mordecai is one of these men.

As a follower of God, Mordecai recognized that God's plan to save His people would come through his niece. He knew that God had prepared Esther and arranged the details of her life for exactly this moment.

He didn't think, *"We need a man for this job."* Instead, he knew that his girl, his adopted daughter, was the one God had chosen.

So he challenged her.

He encouraged her and said, *"You can do this...you have to do this."*

He supported her by organizing the prayer and fasting. He was her cheerleader on the sidelines, saying, *"You can do this. God will help you, and you can save God's people."*

This is the heart and attitude of every unbreakable man of God.

Here's the thing: Because an unbreakable man has already dealt with any brokenness inside of them, they are not afraid of strong women. They don't see women as competition or a threat. Rather, they genuinely love their wives, daughters, mothers, and sisters (including sisters in Christ), and they want to see them reach the full potential God has for them.

They aren't intimidated when a woman succeeds. Instead, they are proud of them. They encourage the women in their lives to take the class, learn new things, use their talents, take risks, step into the opportunity, and do everything God has called them to do.

They know that in God's kingdom, men and women are both called to serve and support each other. When both men and women are free to step into God's callings for their lives, God's kingdom and relationships prosper. So, they encourage and support the women around them to do all that God calls them to do.

When we read the book of Esther, we see that the salvation of the Jewish people began with one man who said, *"My girl can do it."*

Do you have this attitude toward the women in your life?

Are you an unbreakable man who wants to see your wife, daughter, and all the women in your life become everything God created them to be and do everything He has called them to do?

Will you follow in the footsteps of Mordecai and, more importantly, Jesus and support, encourage, challenge, and cheer for the women in your life?

Do you have this type of unbreakable love and courage?

If the answer is *"no,"* what practical steps will you take to become this unbreakable man?

The fact is that God never intended for men and women to work against each other, to compete with each other, or try to dominate each other. In God's kingdom, men and women are equal. Everyone is born with talents, abilities, and gifts designed to follow God's path for their lives.

We can be like Jesus (and Mordecai) when we allow the women in our lives the freedom to be who they are, grow, and shine in whatever area God leads them. By working together and serving each other, we can end the battle of the sexes and become a strong, unbreakable team.

SUNDAY
☐ Psalms 116-118

MONDAY
☐ Jeremiah 4-6

☐ 2 Corinthians 2

TUESDAY
☐ Jeremiah 7-8

☐ 2 Corinthians 3

WEDNESDAY
☐ Jeremiah 9-10

☐ 2 Corinthians 4

THURSDAY
☐ Jeremiah 11-12

☐ 2 Corinthians 5

FRIDAY
☐ Jeremiah 13-14

☐ 2 Corinthians 6

NOTES AND REFLECTION

MEMORY VERSE

But I discipline my body and keep it under control, lest after preaching to others I myself should be disqualified. -1 Corinthians 9:27

Week Thirty-Nine

HE AIN'T GETTING KILLED; HE'S GETTING MAD![1] -PAULIE

In *Rocky III*, Rocky fights Mr. T's character, Clubber Lang. In their first fight, Clubber knocks Rocky out. Then Apollo Creed decides to train Rocky and teach him how to fight and beat Clubber in a rematch.

Apollo teaches Rocky how to fight and be a boxer, including footwork, avoiding punches, and so on. Eventually, Rocky picks it up, and the rematch is on.

Up until this point, Rocky couldn't handle losing the first fight. He felt defeated, and he was scared of Clubber. He thought Clubber was stronger than he was, which was true. He carried himself in a defeated manner.

But then the fight starts, and Rocky uses all the teaching Apollo has taught him. Because of that, Clubber couldn't hit Rocky. But then, as Rocky is halfway through the fight, Clubber lays a massive punch on Rocky. But instead of going down and staying down, Rocky gets back up and keeps fighting, realizing now he can take the punches that Clubber throws at him.

Rocky starts letting Clubber flail away at him as the fight goes on. It looks like Rocky is getting beat. Even Apollo thinks so and says to Paulie, *"He's getting killed out there."*[1]

But in a rare moment when Paulie knows more than Apollo, he says, *"No, he ain't getting killed; he's getting mad!"*[1]

Rocky allowed the anger inside to fuel him to victory. How dare Clubber try to take what belonged to him? How dare he try to make Rocky feel defeated and worthless?

Guys, holy anger is a good thing. When the enemy comes at you and starts flailing away, you need to get mad! Instead of crumpling in defeat, get angry! Let a holy anger rise up inside of you.

Who does the enemy think he is to come at you as a son of God?

1 John 4:4 says, ***"You, dear children, are from God and have overcome them, because the one who is in you is greater than the one who is in the world." (NIV)***

Let it light a fire inside of you, stiffen your spine.

FIGHT!

Get to work, push ahead, and leave the victory to God!

We can't let the enemy keep defeating us. When he throws his attacks at us, no matter what the attack may be, we have two choices: roll over and accept the defeat, or stand up, get angry, and fight!

We don't have to keep getting defeated by the enemy. We can turn to God and tell Him all our struggles.

We can rely on friends for support. We can get angry at the enemy's audacity, stand up, move forward, and fight.

An unbreakable man gets angry at sin, attacks, and fights with everything in him to gain victory.

Don't get defeated; get angry and win!

SUNDAY

☐ Psalms 119:1-48

MONDAY

☐ Jeremiah 15-16

☐ 2 Corinthians 7

TUESDAY

☐ Jeremiah 17-19

☐ 2 Corinthians 8

WEDNESDAY

☐ Jeremiah 20-21

☐ 2 Corinthians 9

THURSDAY

☐ Jeremiah 22-24

☐ 2 Corinthians 10

FRIDAY

☐ Jeremiah 25-26

☐ 2 Corinthians 11

NOTES AND REFLECTION

MEMORY VERSE

His was according to the eternal purpose that he has realized in Christ Jesus our Lord in whom we have boldness and access with confidence through our faith in him.
-Ephesians 3:11-12

Week Forty

GENTLEMEN, IT'S BEEN A PRIVILEGE FLYING WITH YOU.[1]
-JIM LOVELL, APOLLO 13

Many who read this line will recognize it from the 1995 movie *Apollo 13*. While it's not a documentary, it retells the story of Jim Lovell, Fred Haise, and Jack Swigert's attempted trip to the moon. They were supposed to have the third lunar landing as part of the Apollo Space Program. Lovell and Haise were supposed to be the fifth and sixth men ever to walk on the moon. However, when an oxygen tank onboard exploded about fifty-six hours into their flight, everything changed. Their new mission was survival—getting back to earth alive.

One of the saddest scenes in the movie is when Lovell can see the moon through the window and realizes his dream of walking on the moon is gone. Yet, being a leader, he has his moment, refocuses, and says, *"Gentlemen, what are your intentions? I'd like to go home."*[1]

To do this, they'd have to work together. Even though Lovell and Haise weren't happy that Swigert replaced their friend, Ken Mattingly, on the flight, working together became essential. Quickly, they had to push aside playing blame games or personality differences and work as a team because they needed each other.

In the scene where they had to do a *"manual burn"* to get the ship back on course, each man had a job they had to do. They couldn't reenter the earth's atmosphere if one made a mistake. They had to work together with precision and timing to hit their exact target.

When Haise got sick, he needed encouragement from the other men.

When one man's brain got confused and made incorrect calculations, a friend helped him see the mistake.

For better or for worse, they were in this together.

But they weren't alone. Back in Houston, everyone's attention turned to saving the lives of the astronauts on board. And I mean everyone.

Getting these astronauts back home was a team effort.

As you watched the movie, you saw that while the astronauts initially received all the publicity for going to the moon, it took everyone working together to get them back home safely.

The guys in the command center, the mathematicians, engineers, doctors, and many others worked around the clock to bring the astronauts home. One of my favorite lines from the movie is when one of the geeky engineers figures out how to make a square object fit in a round hole to create an air filter so the astronauts don't run out of air. Someone turns to him and says, *"You, sir, are a steely-eyed missile man."*[1]

Then there was the guy who should have been in space but wasn't. Ken Mattingly. His mission was scrubbed when it was suspected that he might have the measles just before take-off.

He was understandably angry after losing his dream of going to the moon. Yet, what no one knew at the time was that this mistake was actually *"providential"* because it was ultimately his knowledge, his experience, and all of the training he received as he prepared to go on the mission that enabled him to create a plan to power up the ship and bring the men back home safely.

Even though he wasn't where he wanted to be (flying to the moon), he was vital to the team. Because of his plan and the work of every other team member, the story had a happy ending. The astronauts got home safely.

While this movie (and the real-life story) could teach us many things about being an unbreakable man, one of the most important lessons we see is that no man is an island. We cannot survive life alone.

We need other people to support us, encourage us, and lend their perspectives, advice, and expertise. We need those who have gone before us to tell us their stories so that we can learn from them. Then, we can provide that same support to those who come after us.

We need people who will stand with us in the hard times like Lovell did when Haise was sick. We need people who will pray, remind us why we do what we do, and encourage us to go forward.

We need others who will correct us like Swigert did when Haise made an error in calculation to tell us, *"Dude, you're headed in the wrong direction; you need to adjust."*

We need men like Lovell who demonstrate leadership. Men like Mattingly who show true loyalty and friendship even when it doesn't benefit them.

And we need everyone—even the guy who might usually go unnoticed but becomes the steely-eyed missile man when he does what no one else can.

As Christian men, we need our band of brothers because together, we are strong. Alone, we will quickly falter and break.

Ecclesiastes 4:9-12 puts it this way:

> ***Two are better than one, because they have a good return for their labor: If either of them falls down, one***

can help the other up. But pity anyone who falls and has no one to help them up.

Also, if two lie down together, they will keep warm. But how can one keep warm alone? Though one may be overpowered, two can defend themselves. A cord of three strands is not quickly broken. (NIV)

So here's the question: Do you have a band of brothers?

Right now, today, to whom would you say, *"Gentlemen, it's been a privilege flying with you?"* [1]

Today is a good day to text or call them and tell them you appreciate them.

If you don't have men like this, I challenge you to start planning to find a band of brothers.

A great place to start is by attending your local men's group. If your church doesn't have one, start one.

Ask God to help you find your band of brothers, guys who do life with you and help you all become unbreakable.

SUNDAY
☐ Psalms 119:49-96

MONDAY
☐ Jeremiah 27-28

☐ 2 Corinthians 12

TUESDAY
☐ Jeremiah 29-30

☐ 2 Corinthians 13

WEDNESDAY
☐ Jeremiah 31-33

☐ 1 John 1

THURSDAY
☐ Jeremiah 34-36

☐ 1 John 2

FRIDAY
☐ Jeremiah 37-39

☐ 1 John 3

NOTES AND REFLECTION

MEMORY VERSE

So I ask you not to lose heart over what I am suffering for you, which is your glory.
-Ephesians 3:13

Week Forty-One

OH, YOU GET THROUGH THAT, AND YOU FIND THE ONLY KIND OF RESPECT THAT MATTERS IN THIS WORLD: SELF-RESPECT. -MARTIN, ROCKY BALBOA

One of the biggest traps men face today is trying to gain other people's respect. Men want respect; they need it. They want to be thought of as good men, winners, and champions. However, no one can give you what you really need: self-respect.

One of my favorite movies is *Rocky Balboa*, from 2006. Maybe it's because I am getting older, but every time I watch it, the story resonates with me more and more. The movie focuses on an aging, grieving Rocky, but in this devotional, let's look at the young boxer he will eventually face, Mason Dixon.

Mason is the undisputed Heavyweight Champion of the World, but no one respects him or the title because he never really fought a tough fight to get it. He hates the disrespect he faces and wants people to appreciate his successes. Fed up with it, he goes to visit his old trainer. What follows is a great scene!

Martin: You got everything money can buy, except what it can't. Its Pride. Pride is what got your {butt} out here, and losing is what brought ya back. But people like you, they need to be tested. They need a challenge.

Mason Dixon: But you know that ain't never gunna happen, there ain't anybody out there Martin.

Martin: There's always somebody out there. Always. And when that time comes and you find something standing if front of you, something that ain't running and ain't backin up and is hittin on you and your too…tired to breathe. You find that situation on you, that good, Cuz thats baptizim under fire! Oh you get thru that and you find the only kind of respect that matters in this world, Self respect.[1] (edited for language)

Martin knew that Mason wouldn't gain the respect of others until he respected himself.

Mason meets that force that doesn't back down when he faces off against Rocky. It is a brutal fight until the end, but Mason stands through it and continues to fight Rocky. He doesn't break as many predicted he would when facing a brutal test.

Instead, he stood and fought, and for the first time in his career, he felt the feeling of respecting himself for his efforts as he stood toe to toe with an opponent and won. This is a crucial part of becoming an unbreakable man.

To be unbreakable, you must respect yourself enough to fight against the sins and traps that entangle you. You must fight with everything you have because you know you are worthy to be called a child of God, and you want to live like such a man.

You respect your identity in Christ enough to stand against sexual temptation.

You fight back against fear because you know God defeated fear; what can man do to you? (Psalm 118:6)

You destroy anger and rage in your life, knowing God created you to live a life of power, love, and a sound mind. (2 Timothy 1:7)

You fight against any weapon formed against you because you know that He Who is in you is greater than He who is in the world. (Isaiah 54:17 and 1 John 4:4)

When you face these battles, when you find something standing in front of you, *"something that ain't running and ain't backin' up and is hittin' on you, and you're too tired to breathe, and you get these victories, you will begin to recognize the man of God that you have become."* This will bring self-respect to you so that you don't care what others think. All that matters is what God thinks of you and what you think of yourself. When this is your focus, you will be a champion.

This is the mindset of an unbreakable man.

SUNDAY
- [ ] Psalms 119:97-136

MONDAY
- [ ] Jeremiah 40-42
- [ ] 1 John 4

TUESDAY
- [ ] Jeremiah 43-45
- [ ] 1 John 5

WEDNESDAY
- [ ] Jeremiah 46-48
- [ ] 2 John 1

THURSDAY
- [ ] Jeremiah 49-50
- [ ] 3 John 1

FRIDAY
- [ ] Jeremiah 51-52
- [ ] Jude 1

NOTES AND REFLECTION

MEMORY VERSE

For this reason I bow my knees before the Father, from whom every family in heaven and on earth is named. -Ephesians 3:14-15

Week Forty-Two

THOUGH THE FIG TREE SHOULD NOT BLOSSOM, NOR FRUIT BE ON THE VINES, THE PRODUCE OF THE OLIVE FAIL AND THE FIELDS YIELD NO FOOD, THE FLOCK BE CUT OFF FROM THE FOLD AND THERE BE NO HERD IN THE STALLS, YET I WILL REJOICE IN THE LORD; I WILL TAKE JOY IN THE GOD OF MY SALVATION. GOD, THE LORD, IS MY STRENGTH; HE MAKES MY FEET LIKE THE DEER'S; HE MAKES ME TREAD ON MY HIGH PLACES. -HABAKKUK 3:17-19 (ESV)

"Say what??"

"Excuse me?"

"I couldn't have heard that right."

"Whatcha talkin' bout Willis?"[1]

Okay, you have to be of a certain age group to get that last one, but they all mean the same thing—Habakkuk could not believe God's reply to his prayer. He was shocked.

But first, let's ask, *"Who in the heck is Habakkuk?"*

Habakkuk was a prophet in Judah. He lived before the people of Judah were taken captive by the Babylonians. The Israelites were already taken captive by the Assyrians because they rejected God and His laws.

Unfortunately, the people of Judah didn't see what happened to their Israelite brothers and think, *"We should stop sinning and turn back to God."* Instead, they continued worshipping idols and rejecting God's ways. Even though under King Josiah, Judah made a lot of progress toward turning back to God, after his death, they returned to their old idol worship ways. Brokenhearted about this spiritual state of his country, Habakkuk went to God in prayer and said, *"Why aren't you doing anything about this?" (Habakkuk 1:1-4)*

But here's the thing: like many who pray for their country, Habakkuk was praying for revival. He wanted the country to turn back to God, to change their ways, and to start following Him. He wanted things to get better.

That's why God's reply completely shocked him. As we read in verses 5-11, God told Habakkuk, *"I'm going to do something. I'm sending the Babylonians to Judah into captivity so they can see their sin, repent, and change."*

You can almost hear Habakkuk scream, *"NOOOOOOO!"*

That was the last thing Habakkuk wanted. The Babylonians were brutal, murderous people. He wanted his country to be saved, but the Babylonians would destroy it. How could this be?

As we continue to read Habakkuk, we see God continue to lay out His plan.

Yes, the Babylonians will conquer Judah because that is the only way that Judah will take their idolatry seriously and turn back to Him.

But—there's more.

After some time, God will then punish the Babylonians for their wickedness, including what they will do to Judah.

After captivity, God's people will again return to Him.

As we know, this is what happened. But can you imagine being Habakkuk and hearing this news?

He was devastated. This was the nightmare—the thing you hoped never happened, and yet it was going to happen.

How did Habakkuk go on?

How did he continue following God?

How did he face this future?

We see his response in chapter 3 as he prays:

> *O Lord, I have heard the report of you, and your work, O Lord, do I fear.*
>
> *In the midst of the years revive it; in the midst of the years make it known; in wrath remember mercy. -Habakkuk 3:1-2 (ESV)*

We see Habakkuk's honesty when he says,

> *I hear, and my body trembles; my lips quiver at the sound; rottenness enters into my bones; my legs tremble beneath me.*
>
> *Yet I will quietly wait for the day of trouble to come upon people who invade us. -Habakkuk 3:16 (ESV)*

And then we have this quote:

> *Though the fig tree should not blossom, nor fruit be on the vines,*
>
> *the produce of the olive fail and the fields yield no food,*

the flock be cut off from the fold and there be no herd in the stalls,

yet I will rejoice in the Lord; I will take joy in the God of my salvation.

God, the Lord, is my strength; he makes my feet like the deer's; he makes me tread on my high places.
-Habakkuk 3:17-19 (ESV)

Here, we see an example of an unbreakable man of God responding when the worst happens.

We see he was honest with God—he didn't like it.

He admitted that he was afraid—he didn't deny his feelings.

Yet, in the end, he knew that his hope was built on God no matter how bad things got, no matter how much he lost or how much he went through.

He found joy in his salvation and turned to God for strength.

He knew God would enable Him to endure the most difficult times as they walked together.

Here's the thing: I don't like bad news.

There are times in life when I ask God, *"Why? Why can't you make a different choice? I don't like Your way. Can't we do it differently?"*

If we're honest, we all have those days.

But here's the thing: Habakkuk demonstrates that having the feeling or asking the question doesn't mean we are broken. It means we are human.

What makes us unbreakable is our dependence, our trust in an unbreakable God, and our belief that no matter what He chooses to allow us to go through, He will give us the strength, agility, tenacity, and perseverance to walk through it with Him.

As we walk together with Him, we are unbreakable.

SUNDAY

☐ Psalms 119:137-176

MONDAY

☐ 1 Chronicles 10-11

☐ Romans 1

TUESDAY

☐ 1 Chronicles 12-13

☐ Romans 2

WEDNESDAY

☐ 1 Chronicles 14-15

☐ Romans 3

THURSDAY

☐ 1 Chronicles 16-17

☐ Romans 4

FRIDAY

☐ 1 Chronicles 18-19

☐ Romans 5

NOTES AND REFLECTION

MEMORY VERSE

According to the riches of his glory he may grant you to be strengthened with power through his Spirit in your inner being.
-Ephesians 3:16

Week Forty-Three

I MADE A COVENANT WITH MY EYES NOT TO LOOK LUSTFULLY AT A YOUNG WOMAN. -JOB

The Book of Job is such a fascinating book of the Bible. It tells the story of a man named Job. Job was rich, had a great family, and his servants loved him. Dude was living in Fat City as he served and followed God. The Bible says Job was the most loyal and faithful follower of God in his time. This fact doesn't go unnoticed by Satan.

Satan goes to God and says the only reason Job serves Him is because God blesses him. God disagrees and tells Satan he can prove it. God allows Satan to come against Job as long as Satan doesn't kill him. He knew Job would stay loyal to Him in bad and good times.

So Satan goes out and starts his assault on Job.

In about an hour, Job loses EVERYTHING.

Enemies attacked and stole his cattle, killing his servants in the process.

A freak lightning storm stuck and destroyed all of his sheep and livestock.

Simultaneously, a second enemy attacked and destroyed every camel he owned.

Amazingly, as all of this went on, a tornado came and destroyed the home where his children were all gathered, burying them dead in the rubble. What a horrible day!

If there had ever been a man who should have been angry and disappointed in God, it would have been Job! What a horrible 24 hours! The Bible makes it clear it all happened with God's permission. God chose to allow Job to lose everything! But Job refused to sin against God!

Even when his *"friends"* came to cheer him up by telling him he was an awful man who deserved everything he got (with friends like that, who needed enemies), Job never turned on God.

Job didn't even turn on God when his beloved wife submitted her entry for *"Wife of the Year"* when she told him to give up, curse God, and die.

Through it all, Job stood firm. God used it to bring glory to himself, burn some spiritual pride out of Job, and make him an even better man of God. The book of Job ends with him having more kids (I guess he worked through the whole *"just die"* thing), more riches, and greater honor. It really is a good book about an unbreakable man.

Tucked in the story of Job is a nugget we can't just skip past. One of the things that made Job such an unbreakable man was his refusal to sin against God. He made it a point to safeguard against the biggest sin men struggle with... lust.

> ***I made a covenant with my eyes not to look lustfully at a young woman. -Job 31:1 (NIV)***

One of the quickest ways the enemy destroys men is through lust and pornography. It is his go-to play. It is his *"Derrick Henry middle-dive run"* (try and stop it in *Madden*). Satan uses it repeatedly and has too much success with it. But notice, he never went that way to try and destroy Job. You'd think it'd be his first attack, but he never used it. Why?

Because he knew it wouldn't work. He knew Job had made a conscious decision to stay pure and to guard his eyes and heart. What a testimony!

Men of God, we need to make this same decision as Job. An unbreakable man commits that sexual integrity is a must. Giving into our sexual desires isn't even an option. We choose to stand with an iron spine and refuse to entertain it.

It seems like an undoable thing, especially in a hyper-sexualized society. *"Greater is he who is in you, than he that is in the world." -1 John 4:4 (KJV)* You can be a man of purity and conviction.

You can look at a woman not as a sexual being but as a daughter of God. You won't want to watch porn because it breaks your heart that someone's daughter is being degraded like this.

You won't ogle a woman in public because you know a man of God should look at a woman as a spiritual sister. (1 Timothy 5:2)

The decision to make a covenant with your eyes will change how you view women, both in your head and your heart.

It starts with a conscious decision and then requires a daily follow-through. Before long, it becomes who you are, and the temptation won't be able to break your will. You can be an unbreakable man of purity, just like Job.

SUNDAY
☐ Psalms 120-122

MONDAY
☐ 1 Chronicles 20-21
☐ Romans 6

TUESDAY
☐ 1 Chronicles 22-23
☐ Romans 7

WEDNESDAY
☐ 1 Chronicles 28-29
☐ Romans 8

THURSDAY
☐ 2 Chronicles 1-2
☐ Romans 9

FRIDAY
☐ 2 Chronicles 3-4
☐ Romans 10

NOTES AND REFLECTION

MEMORY VERSE

Be sober-minded; be watchful. Your adversary the devil prowls around like a roaring lion, seeking someone to devour. -1 Peter 5:8

Week Forty-Four

AYE, FIGHT, AND YOU MAY DIE. RUN, AND YOU'LL LIVE, AT LEAST A WHILE. AND DYING IN YOUR BEDS MANY YEARS FROM NOW, WOULD YOU BE WILLING TO TRADE ALL THE DAYS FROM THIS DAY TO THAT FOR ONE CHANCE, JUST ONE CHANCE TO COME BACK HERE AND TELL OUR ENEMIES THAT THEY MAY TAKE OUR LIVES, BUT THEY'LL NEVER TAKE OUR FREEDOM![1] -WILLIAM WALLACE, BRAVEHEART

It's an iconic scene from the movie *Braveheart*.

Standing in a line, an army of ragtag fighters carrying their makeshift weapons is ready to fight for their beloved Scotland, but more importantly, for their freedom.

That is until they see the enemy.

Walking boldly in formation, clad in body armor, carrying swords and spears, the sight of the enemy makes them quake in their shoes. Completely intimidated and afraid, the amateur army begins to retreat.

That's when William Wallace appears on the scene and makes his famous speech, including these lines:

"You have come to fight as free men, and free men you are. What would you do without freedom? Will you fight?"

Then, a veteran soldier says: "Fight? Against that? No, we will run, and we will live."

To which Wallace replies: "Aye, fight, and you may die. Run, and you'll live -- at least a while. And dying in your beds many years from now, would you be willing to trade all the days from this day to that for one chance, just one chance to come back here and tell our enemies that they may take our lives, but they'll never take our freedom!!!"[1]

Here's the thing-I've never been a huge fan of *Braveheart*. Still, the Holy Spirit reminded me of this quote during a time when He was calling me into a spiritual battle. He was leading me to face issues of my past that I didn't want to deal with and overcome them once and for all.

Truthfully, it was a battle I didn't want to fight.

I didn't want to drudge up painful memories, relive fears, or face the truth about people I loved. I have no desire to go through the heartache and agony.

I didn't have time to go to a counselor and do the homework they assigned. I definitely didn't want to spend the money.

Realizing the changes I needed to make seemed exhausting, overwhelming, and just too hard.

I didn't want to fight that battle. Honestly, I was afraid to fight it. What if I went down the rabbit hole and couldn't deal with the truth I found? Even more petrifying was the question of who I would be when the work of overcoming my past was over.

Like the men who wanted to run away in *Braveheart*, I wanted to take the easy way out, ignore my past and problems, and move on with life.

Who wants to go through all the work it takes to heal our inner brokenness?

And yet, it's the only way to become an unbreakable man of God.

During this time, the Holy Spirit reminded me of this and asked me: "*What if you don't go through God's healing process?*"

Because here's the thing: tearing down strongholds, finding healing, and becoming a sanctified follower of Jesus is not easy. It's literally a battle with sin.

We can choose not to fight. We can choose to continue being oppressed by influences from our old ways of life, trapped in sin, heartache, and pain. You won't have to remember things you don't want to or face hard truths. You'll never see inside a counselor's office or spend hours journaling about your feelings.

But I wonder if those who make that choice someday don't look back on their lives and say, *"What could have been if I'd let the Holy Spirit do everything He wanted to do in my life? What if I'd been brave enough to let Him blow my mind, tear down every stronghold, remove every sin, and make me into everything He wanted me to be?"*

That *"what if"* made me decide I wouldn't take that chance.

The fact is that I don't want to wake up five, ten, twenty years down the road and think, *"What could God have done with my life if I'd been courageous enough to fight the battle in my mind and overcome? Who would I be? How would my relationships be different? What would have happened if I'd been strong enough to fight?"*

Looking at it from this perspective, I made the same choice as the men in *Braveheart*.

I chose to fight. I decided to do the work. I determined I would do whatever it took to overcome my past, gain healing and deliverance, and live the rest of my life in freedom.

I spent time in prayer and allowed the Holy Spirit to bring up any memories He thought I needed to uncover to be free. I journaled, went to counseling, worked through my emotions, chose to forgive those who hurt me, and allowed the Holy Spirit to show me things I needed to change in my life.

Was it easy? No

Do I regret it? Not for a minute.

Because as William Wallace said, *"What is more valuable than freedom?"*[1]

Freedom from sin, freedom from addiction, freedom from heartache and trauma—it's all worth the price, the risk, and the battle.

Perhaps today, you are standing in your own line of decision. The Holy Spirit is calling you to face your past or even the sins of your present and fight a spiritual battle to gain your freedom.

The choice is up to you. Will you remain captive to the sins that so easily control you and the pain of your past, or will you rise like William Wallace and say, *"I want to be free?"*

Will you have your *Braveheart* moment, wear your spiritual armor, and cry, ***"Freedom!"***

SUNDAY
- [ ] Psalms 123-125

MONDAY
- [ ] 2 Chronicles 5-6
- [ ] Romans 11

TUESDAY
- [ ] 2 Chronicles 7-8
- [ ] Romans 12

WEDNESDAY
- [ ] 2 Chronicles 9-10
- [ ] Romans 13

THURSDAY
- [ ] 2 Chronicles 11-12
- [ ] Romans 14

FRIDAY
- [ ] 2 Chronicles 13-14
- [ ] Romans 15

NOTES AND REFLECTION

MEMORY VERSE

Resist him, firm in your faith, knowing that the same kinds of suffering are being experienced by your brotherhood throughout the world.
-1 Peter 5:9

Week Forty-Five

NO MAN STANDS SO TALL AS WHEN HE STOOPS TO HELP A CHILD.[1] -ABRAHAM LINCOLN

What is the greatest compliment you ever received?

I'm sure some kind words someone spoke to you in your lifetime just popped into your head. We all remember special words that touch our hearts when we hear them.

Being a public figure means you get a lot of compliments, and I have learned to take them with a grain of salt because often they are spoken with ulterior motives. But I remember one time someone said something to me, and I will never forget it because it was such a great compliment.

I had posted a picture on Facebook of myself giving a ride on my mobility scooter to the daughter of one of my friends while we were setting up for a Mantour. A Facebook friend made this comment on the picture.

"You da man Jamie! You take time for the little ones all the way up to us ole geezers!! That's what I appreciate about you!"

I couldn't think of a nicer thing that could have been said to me. The truth is, I love kids. They are so fun, have an innocent outlook on life, and love so genuinely.

Men of God, it's time for us to step up and take an active role in shaping the hearts and minds of our children. It's concerning to see that women teach the majority of Sunday school classes for children.

Teaching children is not solely a woman's responsibility, and it's time for more men to participate in this essential aspect of our community. I appreciate all the hardworking women who serve in Sunday schools teaching kids, but where are the men making a difference in the lives of these children?

Let me say this: It is okay for women to teach adult Sunday school classes, and it's okay for men to teach children's classes. Why is this considered controversial in some churches?

Beyond Sunday School, the Royal Rangers program is an excellent opportunity for godly men to invest in the lives of younger men who need a positive role model. While you're teaching them to hunt, fish, and camp, you can also teach them how to love Jesus, treat others in a godly fashion, and be a man of God.

Jesus was a huge kid guy. He loved being around kids, laughing and talking to them. He rebuked His disciples when they kept the kids away from Him (Matthew 19:14). He said that we should all have the humility of a child (Matthew 18:3). He even said a man who causes a child to fall into sin would be better of cast into the ocean with a millstone tied around his neck, the equivalent of a modern-day pair of cement shoes. (Matthew 18:6).

I 100% agree with old Honest Abe. There is no bigger man than one who bends down and makes a child important.

Men, how are you investing in children's lives? Are you the man at church all the kids run up to talk to, or are you the one they hide from because they are scared of you?

Follow Jesus' and honest Abe's words, and become a man who prioritizes the smallest of the world. Let them know they matter to you. Listen to their stories and laugh at their jokes. That is the heart of an unbreakable man, caring for the smallest among us.

SUNDAY

☐ Psalms 126-128

MONDAY

☐ 2 Chronicles 15-16

☐ Romans 16

TUESDAY

☐ 2 Chronicles 17-18

☐ Luke 1

WEDNESDAY

☐ 2 Chronicles 19-20

☐ Luke 2

THURSDAY

☐ 2 Chronicles 21-22

☐ Luke 3

FRIDAY

☐ 2 Chronicles 23-24

☐ Luke 4

NOTES AND REFLECTION

MEMORY VERSE

It is the Lord who goes before you. He will be with you; he will not leave you or forsake you. Do not fear or be dismayed. -Deuteronomy 31:8

Week Forty-Six

PETER PARKER: I JUST WANTED TO BE LIKE YOU. TONY STARK: AND I WANTED YOU TO BE BETTER [1]

Tony Stark. Iron Man. One of the greatest all-time characters in the Marvel movies.

In *Iron Man 1*, we see his transformation from a *"Genius, Billionaire, Playboy, Philanthropist"*[2] to a superhero after he survives terrorists' captivity in a cave. Eventually, we see him move from Superhero to Avenger as he joins the team and saves the world by carrying the nuclear bomb into space.

Later, we see him as the head of the Avengers, providing funding and leadership for the team. Yet, all the while, he maintains that charming, sarcastic wit that we all know and love.

However, when he said the words in today's quote, Tony Stark was in a new and different role—mentor.

The quote comes from *Spider-Man: Homecoming*. Stark's character is a little older and a little wiser, and after recruiting Peter Parker to fight with the Avengers in *Captain America: Civil War*, Tony now feels a sense of responsibility to mentor him and help him in life.

If you've seen *Spider-Man: Homecoming.*, you know that, throughout the movie, Peter struggles with a common issue for young men. He thinks he knows more than he does and is ready for more than he is.

Tony Stark knows this and tells Peter to go home and be a *"friendly neighborhood Spider-Man."*[1]

But Peter has fought with the Avengers. He doesn't want to go home, go to school, and live like a teenager—he wants to be an Avenger.

So, rather than following Tony's advice, Peter continues getting himself into all kinds of trouble. Eventually, he gets in over his head and botches the mission he designed, endangering many innocent people.

Of course, Iron Man flies in and saves the day. Using his superpowers, he saves everyone's life. Then, he turns his attention to Peter. It's time for a bit of correction.

Peter's excuse, *"I wanted to be just like you."*

To which Tony replies, *"But I wanted you to be better."*[1]

What a great quote! What an incredible heart for a mentor.

You see, even though Tony Stark had an extraordinary life, he'd done amazing things, and he had everything anyone could ever want, he also had regrets.

In *Captain America: Civil War*, we see that he wishes he'd have apologized to his dad and made things right before his parents were killed. He carries the burden of all the innocents who died in Sokovia. *Iron Man 3* (the worst of all the Iron Man movies) shows that he struggled with PTSD from all the things he'd seen and been through.

Stark wanted to spare Peter some of these regrets.

He didn't want Peter to be just a great Superhero. He wanted him to become a good man.

So he tried to teach him the fundamentals, hoping that someday Peter wouldn't just take his place, but he'd be a better man with fewer regrets.

He wanted Peter to know that behind the glory, fame, adrenaline rush, and adventure, he needed to have character and a moral code and understand what he was risking everything to defend. He worked tirelessly with Peter—even taking away his suit—so that Peter would learn this lesson.

Whenever I watch this movie, I think about the example this sets in the mentor/mentee relationships.

I'm reminded of 1 Peter 5, which tells older and younger men how to make the most of these relationships. He starts with the *"elders."*

> *To the elders among you, I appeal as a fellow elder and a witness of Christ's sufferings who also will share in the glory to be revealed:*
>
> *Be shepherds of God's flock that is under your care, watching over them—not because you must, but because you are willing, as God wants you to be; not pursuing dishonest gain, but eager to serve; not lording it over those entrusted to you, but being examples to the flock.*
>
> *And when the Chief Shepherd appears, you will receive the crown of glory that will never fade away. -1 Peter 5:1-4 (NIV)*

Paul points out that it is the responsibility of those who are older to shepherd those who are younger. They shouldn't just teach them with words, but they should *"watch over them."* They should help them grow in their faith and become the men they were meant to be.

Part of this means taking the attitude of Tony Stark and *"wanting them to be better."*

Don't be threatened by their youth or abilities, but pour into them, hoping they will learn from your wisdom and experience and ultimately surpass you in God's kingdom.

Then, Paul turns his attention to the younger crowd, the Peter Parkers of the church):

> *In the same way, you who are younger, submit yourselves to your elders. All of you, clothe yourselves with humility toward one another, because,*
>
> *"God opposes the proud but shows favor to the humble."*
>
> *Humble yourselves, therefore, under God's mighty hand, that he may lift you up in due time. -1 Peter 5:5-6 (NIV)*

He's basically saying, "*Dudes, for heaven's sake, listen to the elders. Accept that they know more than you. Don't be arrogant and rebellious and think you know everything. Be humble and admit that you have a lot to learn.*"

Notice that Paul stresses *"humility"* as a critical aspect for mentees. He says that submitting to those trying to teach you shows humility toward your mentor and God.

Another interesting part of humility is trusting that God will exalt you *"in due time."*

Can I just be honest for a moment?

One of the biggest pitfalls I see in too many young men is what I call *"Peter Parker Syndrome."* With stars in their eyes, they believe they are ready for the big promotion NOW. They want to be Tony Stark without ever spending time in the cave. They want glory, promotion, and position without working hard to gain character and learn the fundamentals.

It always ends the same way—badly.

That's why Paul warns us against worrying about when God will exalt us and tells us to focus on humility.

- Take the time.

- Be willing to learn.

- Submit.

- Listen to your mentor.

- Take criticism.

- Love correction.

- Be willing to wait your turn.

Trust that God controls your life. As you humbly submit and do what you're asked to do, God will promote you when He thinks you are ready.

Recognize that neither God nor your mentor wants to hold you back. They both want you to reach your fullest potential and be an unbreakable man of God.

Just like Tony Stark, they want you to be better.

SUNDAY
☐ Psalms 129-131

MONDAY
☐ 2 Chronicles 25-26

☐ Luke 5

TUESDAY
☐ 2 Chronicles 27-28

☐ Luke 6

WEDNESDAY
☐ 2 Chronicles 29-30

☐ Luke 7

THURSDAY
☐ 2 Chronicles 31-32

☐ Luke 8

FRIDAY
☐ 2 Chronicles 33-34

☐ Luke 9

NOTES AND REFLECTION

MEMORY VERSE

I can do all things through him who strengthens me. -Philippians 4:13

Week Forty-Seven

AS GOD AS MY WITNESS I THOUGHT TURKEYS COULD FLY. -THE BIG GUY, MR. CARLSON[1]

I love classic TV, especially holiday episodes. Every Thanksgiving, Adessa and I rewatch old episodes of Thanksgiving-themed TV shows. One of our favorites is *WKRP in Cincinnati's* episode *"Turkeys Away."*

In this episode, Mr. Carlson, the station owner, feels he has become obsolete while the younger staff transitions the station from a news station to a rock and roll station. He doesn't have anything to do while the rest of the staff makes the station hum. He tries to interject himself into the station's inner workings, annoying everyone.

He decides to reinsert himself as the boss and plan a huge Thanksgiving promotion for the station. He only shares his plan with Herb Tarlick and Les Newman, the two employees he hired before the new staff came.

Mr. Carlson sends Les Nessman to do a live-on-air broadcast. We see the staff in the DJ room listening with no clue what is happening. Les does his report. A helicopter circles over a mall parking lot with a banner that says *"Happy Thanksgiving from WKRP"*. Then things get weird.

Les, mimicking the reporters at the Hindenburg disaster reports.:

"Something just came out of the back of a helicopter. It's a dark object, perhaps a skydiver plummeting to the earth from only two thousand feet in the air... There's a third... No parachutes yet... Those

can't be skydivers. I can't tell just yet what they are but... They're turkeys! Oh no!

Oh, they're crashing to the earth right in front of our eyes! One just went through the windshield of a parked car! This is terrible! Everyone's running around pushing each other. Oh my goodness! Oh, the humanity! People are running about. The turkeys are hitting the ground like sacks of wet cement! Folks, I don't know how much longer... The crowd is running for their lives... Children are searching for their mothers, and oh, not since the Hindenburg tragedy has there been anything like this. I don't know how much longer I can hold my position here, Johnny. The crowd..."[1]

The radio goes silent at this point, leaving everyone wondering what happened. DJ Johnny Fever ends it by saying, *"Thanks for that on-the-spot report, Les. For those of you who've just tuned in, the Pinedale Shopping Mall has just been bombed with live turkeys. Film at eleven."* [1]

The episode ends with the station being bombarded with angry calls and threats from PETA, other agencies, and government offices. The final words are from a disheveled, stunned, defeated Mr. Carlson saying, *"As God as my witness, I thought turkeys could fly."* (1)

It is a truly hilarious episode!

But a point can be made out of...two actually.

1. Older Men

To my older brothers in Christ, don't be intimidated when the younger generation outdoes you. I firmly believe that, as men, we should want the next generation to outdue us spiritually and in life and do everything we can to help them achieve this.

2. Younger Men

Younger men, the generation before you has so much wisdom and experience. Don't push them aside. Instead, glean all the help and advice you can from them. Use their wisdom and knowledge to help you become an unbreakable man.

Just think of all the turkeys whose lives could have been saved if they had worked together on a Thanksgiving promotion!

Men of God, we are the most unbreakable when we work together and use each other's strengths without letting insecurities or pride get in the way. Happy Thanksgiving!

SUNDAY
☐ Psalms 132-134

MONDAY
☐ 2 Chronicles 35-36

☐ Luke 10

TUESDAY
☐ Malachi 1

☐ Luke 11

WEDNESDAY
☐ Malachi 2

☐ Luke 12

THURSDAY
☐ Malachi 3

☐ Luke 13

FRIDAY
☐ Malachi 4

☐ Luke 14

NOTES AND REFLECTION

MEMORY VERSE

The end of all things is at hand; therefore be self-controlled and sober-minded for the sake of your prayers. -1 Peter 4:7

Week Forty-Eight

I DIDN'T HEAR NO BELL YET, ONE MORE ROUND. -ROCKY

This a phrase you'll hear around our house a lot.

Because my sister speaks fluent *Rocky* (in all fairness, I'm also fluent in *Gilmore Girls*), she knows exactly what it means.

It comes *from Rocky V*—the one with Tommy Gunn.

When Rocky is tired and wants to quit training, his coach, Mick, says, *"I didn't hear no bell yet."*[1] Later, at the movie's end, when Tommy Gun has knocked Rocky to the ground and thinks the fight is over, Rocky gets back up and says, *"I didn't hear no bell yet, one more round."*[1] Then he gets back up, fights again, and wins.

At first, when I started quoting this line, my sister hated it. She'd be annoyed when we were in the middle of a big project or a series of events, when we'd be tired and want to rest or even give up, and I'd say, *"I didn't hear no bell yet."*

Then, one day, she turned the tables on me during tomato canning season. We'd already spent a few days turning basket after basket of tomatoes in sauce or juice or just canned tomatoes that we could eat during the winter. That morning, I woke up exhausted, and my body was aching. (No joke: canning tomatoes is hard work.) Complaining all the way, I was met with the sarcastic reply, *"I didn't hear no bell yet."*

And we kept going because both of us knew what this phrase meant.

You don't quit until the fight is over.

Keep going.

Stop complaining and get back to doing what you're supposed to do.

Did you hear a bell? Then the fight isn't over. We don't give up in the middle of a task just because it's hard or we are tired. Put on your big boy pants and get back in the fight.

Sometimes, I think this is a wake-up call that today's church needs to hear. Too many men of God are breaking before they hear a bell.

But here's the thing: as followers of Christ, we shouldn't expect to hear any bells. Instead, we should listen for trumpets.

> *For the Lord himself will descend from Heaven with a cry of command, with the voice of an archangel, and with the sound of the trumpet of God. And the dead in Christ will rise first.*
>
> *Then we who are alive, who are left, will be caught up together with them in the clouds to meet the Lord in the air, and so we will always be with the Lord.*
>
> *Therefore, encourage one another with these words.*
> *-1 Thessalonians 4:16-18 (ESV)*

These verses talk about the rapture of the church—the day when Jesus will come back to take His followers with Him to Heaven. Notice that the sound of a trumpet will precede it.

When we look at life through the perspective of eternity, we see that this is the end game for believers. We win when we go to Heaven to spend eternity with Jesus.

Until then, our fight continues. Our calling continues.

Part of being an unbreakable man of God means understanding that we are called to continue living for Jesus, living by God's Word, fighting against sin, leading others to Jesus, and disciplining them until we hear a trumpet sound or Jesus calls us home through death.

This is our mission. It's who we are.

We can't give up when hard times come.

We can't become lazy and neglectful in our relationship with God.

We aren't called to be complacent, to make excuses, or to tolerate sin.

We shouldn't just give up and say, *"It's too hard to be a man of God in today's world. It's too difficult to love my wife and kids—have you met them? Witnessing at work is a struggle—they make fun of me. What's the point anyway?"*

The point is that you are called to something more.

God has an amazing plan for your life and a purpose that He wants you to fulfill. There are people in your sphere of influence that only you can reach with the Gospel and things that need to be done that only you can do.

Your life has a mission and a purpose. You have a role to play in God's kingdom.

That is why you don't give up. It's why you keep going, trying, praying, reading your Bible, and sharing your testimony until your last breath…or until you hear the trumpet sound.

Did you hear a trumpet yet? Then it's not over.

Keep going. Keep trying. Keep following Jesus.

As 2 Thessalonians 3:13 says, *"As for you, brothers, do not grow weary in doing good." (ESV)*

Because you didn't hear no bell yet, keep on fighting!

SUNDAY

☐ **Psalms 135-137**

MONDAY

☐ **Isaiah 1-3**

☐ **Luke 15**

TUESDAY

☐ **Isaiah 4-6**

☐ **Luke 16**

WEDNESDAY

☐ **Isaiah 7-8**

☐ **Luke 17**

THURSDAY

☐ **Isaiah 9-10**

☐ **Luke 18**

FRIDAY

☐ **Isaiah 11-12**

☐ **Luke 19**

NOTES AND REFLECTION

MEMORY VERSE

Yet if anyone suffers as a Christian, let him not be ashamed, but let him glorify God in that name.
-1 Peter 4:16

Week Forty-Nine

...ALL I WANNA DO IS GO THE DISTANCE. NOBODY'S EVER GONE THE DISTANCE WITH CREED, AND IF I CAN GO THAT DISTANCE, YOU SEE, AND THAT BELL RINGS AND I'M STILL STANDIN', I'M GONNA KNOW FOR THE FIRST TIME IN MY LIFE, SEE, THAT I WEREN'T JUST ANOTHER BUM FROM THE NEIGHBORHOOD. -ROCKY[1]

Rocky said these words shortly before his big break fight with Apollo Creed. Rocky had no right to be in the ring with Creed, and everyone knew it. Yet Rocky wanted to show everyone wrong. Rocky's desire to *"go the distance"* should be the desire of all unbreakable men.

As Christian men, we are called to press on toward our heavenly goal, like Rocky sought to prove his worth by enduring the fight. Our ultimate prize is not measured in earthly praise or fame but in our faithful walk with Christ. The Apostle Paul's words in Philippians 3:14 remind us of this pursuit: *"I press on toward the goal to win the prize for which God has called me heavenward in Christ Jesus." (NIV)*

Rocky's determination to go the distance with Creed is a great illustration of this verse and how we must strive to develop perseverance. The Christian journey is filled with challenges, temptations, and obstacles that test our faith and resolve. In James 1:12, we are encouraged, *"Blessed is the one who perseveres under trial because, having stood the test, that person will receive the crown of life that the Lord has promised to those who love him." (NIV)*

We must press on, not for a champion belt, but for a spiritual crown, an eternity in Heaven with God.

One part of this quote that really resonates is Rocky's fear of being *"just another bum."* I think we all have a deep desire for significance. We all struggle with our identity and worth. However, for a man of God, our value cannot be determined by our accomplishments but by our identity in Christ.

We are God's sons! We aren't bums; we are sons of God, and our Father will help us go the distance.

We can stand firm in our faith regardless of life's circumstances. While Rocky sought identity through his fight, we seek an eternal prize. We seek to be unbreakable men who love and serve God until our last breath and then enter into Heaven to be with our Father. This reassurance of the importance of faith in all circumstances should make us feel steadfast and unwavering in our journey.

Men, let's follow Rocky's determination to go the distance. We will persevere through trials, find our identity in Christ, endure the hard times faithfully following God, and keep our eyes fixed on our heavenly prize. When the final bell rings, we will stand firm in our faith, knowing we have fought the good fight and kept the faith as unbreakable men. At that moment, we won't hear anything about being a bum. We will instead hear, ***"Well done, good and faithful servant".***

SUNDAY
☐ Psalms 138-140

MONDAY
☐ Isaiah 13-14

☐ Luke 20

TUESDAY
☐ Isaiah 15-17

☐ Luke 21

WEDNESDAY
☐ Isaiah 18-20

☐ Luke 22

THURSDAY
☐ Isaiah 21-23

☐ Luke 23

FRIDAY
☐ Isaiah 24-26

☐ Luke 24

NOTES AND REFLECTION

MEMORY VERSE

Therefore let those who suffer according to God's will entrust their souls to a faithful Creator while doing good. -1 Peter 4:19

Week Fifty

YEAH, BUT I'VE BEEN DOWN HERE BEFORE AND I KNOW THE WAY OUT. -LEO MCGARRY, THE WEST WING

One of my all-time favorite episodes of *The West Wing* is a Christmas episode, *Noel*. Even though it was a holiday episode, one of the main characters, Josh, was not feeling holly and jolly. Instead, he was experiencing intense PTS episodes from a shooting incident that almost killed him. However, he didn't understand that it was post-traumatic stress. He had no idea what was happening or why he was responding in such unusual ways, including at one point screaming, *"Listen to me"* at the President.

Although he didn't know how to help himself, his boss, Leo, did. Leo brought in a highly trained trauma therapist. Most of the episode centers on the therapy session that explained that whenever Josh heard music, his brain interpreted it as sirens, causing him to relive the trauma of the shooting. Since it was Christmas time at the White House, music was everywhere. It was a fascinating episode—totally worth watching.

Today's quote was from the very end of the episode.

The therapy session was over, and Josh received his diagnosis. One of his first concerns was, *"Can I keep my job?"* (He had a very high-level position and wasn't sure someone with PTS could keep it.)

That's when he sees his boss, Leo, who tells him this story:

"This guy's walking down the street when he falls in a hole. The walls are so steep he can't get out.

A doctor passes by and the guy shouts up, 'Hey you. Can you help me out?' The doctor writes a prescription, throws it down in the hole, and moves on.

Then a priest comes along, and the guy shouts up,

'Father, I'm down in this hole. Can you help me out?'

The priest writes out a prayer, throws it down in the hole, and moves on.

Then a friend walks by, 'Hey, Joe, it's me can you help me out?' And the friend jumps in the hole.

Our guy says, 'Are you stupid? Now we're both down here.'

The friend says, 'Yeah, but I've been down here before and I know the way out.'"[1]

Leo then assures Josh that as long as he's there, Josh will have a job. However, you need to know Leo's background to understand the story.

You see, Leo was a recovering alcoholic. Having been through his own hard times, he recognized that Josh needed help and got it for him. He'd been down a hard road before, and now he would help another man during his difficult time.

In this scene, Leo sets an example that all unbreakable men of God can follow. Because all around us, people are struggling, suffering, and going through hard times.

As an unbreakable man of God, you can use your testimony—the things God has brought you through to help them.

But here's the thing—too many men of God are afraid to share their testimony. They're worried their reputation will be ruined if people discover who they were or what they did. More concerned about what others think than helping another person, they keep their testimony to themselves.

Yet, they are so misinformed.

The fact is that sharing your testimony makes you stronger. First, it takes courage to share. Like a muscle, courage is strengthened the more it is used.

Secondly, after you've told your *"big story"* a few times and realized that no one is shocked, no one thinks less of you, or that it helps another person more than it hurts you, it shatters the lie that it will destroy you. Once that lie is gone, you'll want to share again.

Third, sharing your testimony reminds you of what God has done. When you see how the Holy Spirit uses your testimony to change another person's life, it gives you even more evidence of God's power. It's exciting to be a part of what God is doing and see another man changed.

Finally, you'll have killed the pride that wants to keep everything a secret and protect your image. Have no doubt—that's what's keeping you from sharing. More than fear, you don't want to look bad—it's pride.

Yet, the Bible says that pride goes before a fall.

> ***Pride goes before destruction, and haughtiness before a fall. -Proverbs 16:18 (NLT)***

So, ultimately, you can choose whether to smash your pride or allow your pride to break you.

Here's a secret: when you kill your pride, share your testimony, and help someone else, you'll experience freedom like never before.

With the pride gone, you'll have an unbreakable testimony that can say, *"Yeah, I've been there, but I know that Jesus is the answer."*

SUNDAY
☐ Psalms 141-143

MONDAY
☐ Isaiah 27-29

☐ Mark 1

TUESDAY
☐ Isaiah 30-32

☐ Mark 2

WEDNESDAY
☐ Isaiah 33-35

☐ Mark 3

THURSDAY
☐ Isaiah 36-38

☐ Mark 4

FRIDAY
☐ Isaiah 39-41

☐ Mark 5

NOTES AND REFLECTION

MEMORY VERSE

Count it all joy, my brothers, when you meet trials of various kinds, for you know that the testing of your faith produces steadfastness. And let steadfastness have its full effect, that you may be perfect and complete, lacking in nothing.
-James 1:2-4

Week Fifty-One

THAT'S WHAT CHRISTMAS MEMORIES ARE MADE FROM, THEY'RE NOT PLANNED, THEY'RE NOT SCHEDULED, NOBODY PUTS THEM IN THEIR BLACKBERRY, THEY JUST HAPPEN. [1] -KELLY FINCH, DECK THE HALLS

It's one of the great Christmas classics.

Two neighbors, who both love Christmas, fall into the trap of competing to be the *King of Christmas* in the neighborhood.

On the one hand, you've got Buddy, the new guy in the neighborhood who is going through some mid-life crisis. He is trying to find his identity and purpose in life by putting so many Christmas lights on his house that it can be seen from space.

On the other side of the street, there's Steve Finch. Before Buddy arrives in town, he's known as *Mr. Christmas.* He loves the holidays —as long as everything goes his way and follows his traditional, this-is-how-to-have-the-perfect-Christmas checklist. He's even got an Advent Calendar full of *"things to do"* during the season.

There's a rivalry as soon as they meet—mostly because Steve feels that Buddy is stepping on his Christmas turf. Throughout the movie, the competition escalates until Steve finally has enough and decides to purchase illegal fireworks to bomb Buddy's house in the middle of the night. (Yeah, this rivalry is intense.)

Of course, Steve's no expert felon (he's a geeky nerd), and his firework plan backfires and damages his house. That's when his wife Kelly has enough. Packing their kids to spend Christmas in a hotel, they have this conversation:

Kelly Finch: What is your favorite Christmas memory?

Steve Finch: You know what it is.

Kelly Finch: Tell me.

Steve Finch: I was 7, my dad and I moved to Alabama... and Christmas morning we ate on the floor, ate French fries and drank chocolate milk.

Kelly Finch: That's what Christmas memories are made from, they're not planned, they're not scheduled, nobody puts them in their Blackberry, they just happen.[1]

Perhaps we all need to remember this as we approach the next two weeks of Christmas and New Years.

Let's be honest: the holidays can be stressful. If Chevy Chase taught us nothing else in *Christmas Vacation*, he showed us that the combination of crazy relatives and unrealistic expectations can create chaos.

So, before we fall into this Christmas trap, let's step back and remember that Christmas isn't a competition.

It isn't about who buys their kids the best stuff or who gets the latest tech from their wives.

Christmas doesn't have to be perfect.

We don't have to do things as we've always done them.

Things don't always have to be the way you think they should be.

Most importantly, don't bomb your neighbor's house with fireworks if you find their light display offensive. (Okay, that was just for fun.)

Instead, we need to be flexible if we want to remain unbreakable during the holiday season. Like a tree that bends with the wind, we must relax and go with the flow.

We must remember that just as Christ laid down His life for us, as men, we are called to lay down our lives for our families and those around us. (Ephesians 5:25-33 and Ephesians 6:4)

That means sacrifice. Flexibility. Being less annoyed and more excited about the things that excite those around us.

As Steve and Buddy learned at the end of the movie, we need to stop worrying about ourselves and do what is best for those around us. Be the unbreakable man they can rely on, and have a very Merry Christmas.

SUNDAY
- [ ] Psalms 144-146

MONDAY
- [ ] Isaiah 55-56
- [ ] Matthew 1-2

TUESDAY
- [ ] Isaiah 57-58
- [ ] Luke 1

WEDNESDAY
- [ ] Isaiah 59
- [ ] Luke 2

THURSDAY
- [ ] Isaiah 60
- [ ] Mark 11

FRIDAY
- [ ] Isaiah 61-62
- [ ] Mark 12

NOTES AND REFLECTION

MEMORY VERSE

As for you, brothers, do not grow weary in doing good. -2 Thessalonians 3:13

Week Fifty-Two

LIVE EVERY DAY UNTIL YOU DIE.

My mentor once shared these words with me, and they really struck a chord with me. He emphasized the importance of not taking life for granted, continually moving forward, taking chances, and living life to its fullest, whether at work or play.

Unbreakable men need to live every day until they die. They don't give up.

One of my favorite Bible men is Caleb, who lived every day with this attitude. Even when Caleb grew old, he had the same passion and fervor for God that He had as a younger man.

Let's look at one of the best passages in the Bible found in Joshua 14:10-

> *And now, behold, the Lord has kept me alive, just as he said, these forty-five years since the time that the Lord spoke this word to Moses, while Israel walked in the wilderness.*
>
> *And now, behold, I am this day eighty-five years old.*
>
> *I am still as strong today as I was in the day that Moses sent me; my strength now is as my strength was then, for war and for going and coming.*
>
> *So now give me this hill country of which the Lord spoke on that day, for you heard on that day how the Anakim were there, with great fortified cities. It may be*

that the Lord will be with me, and I shall drive them out just as the Lord said. (ESV)

The Bible tells us that, well into his 80s, Caleb still fought hard to enter God's promise to him. Instead of staying at home, putting his feet up on a park bench, and feeding the birds all day while his children fought the battles, he strapped on his sword, conquered the enemy himself, and took the land God had promised to him.

Through God's power, he took his Promised Land and conquered a part of the Negev. Being a godly man, he gave this land to his daughter. He supplied her with a worthy husband. He cared for his family and left his daughter a land free from enemies. He didn't stop living until he took his last breath!

I've been blessed to know men like Caleb, whose bodies have grown older, but their passion for God's kingdom has only grown stronger. For instance, I have one elderly friend who needs to spend three days a week on dialysis. But do you know what he does while he's there? He studies the Bible. He prays. He counsels people on the phone. He prepares for the sermons he will preach whenever a church needs a volunteer pastor. Rather than feeling sorry for himself or putting his feet up and saying, *"I've run a good race; now I can relax,"* this man's attitude is, *"Who can I reach for Jesus next?"*

I know another older man who recently said to me that he would explode if one more person asked him when he would retire. He told me he is nowhere near ready for that; he still has too much to do for God and His Kingdom!

I know other men who have retired from their secular jobs and spend their time volunteering at their local churches. Others help raise their grandchildren to become men and women of God. Still, others saw retirement as a time to start a new ministry.

Guys, old age and retirement aren't a time for complacency——it's a time to follow Caleb's example and say, *"I'm still breathing, I'm still on fire for God, what's next?"*

Live 'til you die!!! This is the mark of an unbreakable man: no matter what happens in life or what stage of life you're in, you are grateful to God and follow Him wholeheartedly. This is a man God can use. This is the man I hope you will be inspired to be.

Live every day for Jesus and finish well!

SUNDAY

☐ **Psalms 147-148**

MONDAY

☐ **Isaiah 42-44**

☐ **Mark 6**

TUESDAY

☐ **Isaiah 45-46**

☐ **Mark 7**

WEDNESDAY

☐ **Isaiah 47-48**

☐ **Mark 8**

THURSDAY

☐ **Isaiah 49-52**

☐ **Mark 9**

FRIDAY

☐ **Isaiah 53-55**

☐ **Mark 10**

NOTES AND REFLECTION

MEMORY VERSE

Blessed is the man who remains steadfast under trial, for when he has stood the test he will receive the crown of life, which God has promised to those who love him. -James 1:12

Bonus Week Fifty-Three

BY FAILING TO PREPARE, YOU ARE PREPARING TO FAIL.
-BENJAMIN FRANKLIN

And so we've come to the end of our journey. Whether you've been reading along online or in the devotional book, it's been a lot of fun looking at the different quotes and seeing how we can apply them to our lives to become unbreakable men of God.

As we wrap up, I'd like to issue you one last challenge:

As we head into a New Year this week, I'd like you to take some time, get alone, and ask yourself a few hard questions.

First, what are the three areas in which I am most vulnerable to breaking in my life?

- What are my weak spots?

- Where do I most easily fall into temptation?

- What triggers me to become the man I don't want to be?

I know it's hard, but we must be honest with ourselves. After all, we can only solve a problem once we admit it exists.

Next, I want you to make a prayerful plan.

As you have your devotions this week, ask God to help you create a plan to shore up your weaknesses.

James 1:5 says, *"If you need wisdom, ask our generous God, and he will give it to you. He will not rebuke you for asking." (NLT)*

Because God loves us, He wants to help us become unbreakable men. This includes facing and repairing the areas in our lives that tend to be broken.

I can say without a doubt that as you seek God, the Holy Spirit will show you practical steps to help you create a plan to repair the broken areas, implement new behavioral patterns, and become the unbreakable man of God that you were meant to be.

As the Holy Spirit helps you create a plan:

1. Write it down.

Put it on paper. Keep that paper where you see it often so you're reminded of your plan and commitment.

2. Share it with a trusted godly friend.

Just like a fighter can't win without his team of coaches and supporters around him, so men of God need each other to succeed in the Christian life. After you have your plan, share it with a trusted Christian brother who will hold you accountable. Tell him to check up on you once in a while. Even if you get annoyed, tell him to try again. You may even give him permission to use the phrase, *"I didn't hear no bell yet,"* if you start to give up before you win the fight.

Let him be as brutally honest with you as a coach is with a fighter. When you win the battle, you can celebrate together.

3. Don't give up.

Maybe you're weak in personal Bible reading. Your plan is to choose a Bible reading plan and read a little every day. You're even reading with a friend for accountability.

Then you hit Leviticus, and it's rough. As you struggle to read about sacrifices and dietary laws, you start to think, *"I wonder what's on television."* (Trust me, we've all been there.)

This is the time to remember *Braveheart*, put on your spiritual face paint, and say, "*I'm not giving up!!! God's Word is my key to freedom, and I'm not backing down!*"

Then keep going! Kill your tendency toward laziness, excuses, and complacency, and keep fighting. Stick to your plan. Don't give up.

4. Celebrate the wins, no matter how small.

Sticking to a plan is easier when we stop to celebrate the wins along the way. This is why *AA* gives out chips for even the smallest amounts of time that someone is sober.

As you stick to your plan next year, I encourage you to do the same. Did you have devotions for a week? Congratulate yourself!

Did you go a month without losing your temper? Tell a friend and celebrate together.

One way to do this is to share your testimony and celebrate what God is doing in your life. Remember: every small step gets you closer to your goal. So celebrate.

5. If you fall off the wagon, get back up.

What do you do if you don't stick to your plan, if you fall off the wagon and go backward?

Ask God to forgive you and start following your plan again.

Don't throw out the plan just because you made a mistake.

Don't quit. Get back up, start again, and keep moving toward becoming the unbreakable man God wants you to be.

Always know that I believe you can do it.

But it starts with a plan.

Here's the thing: As I was preparing for this last chapter, I came across three quotes about planning. I had difficulty deciding which one to use, but I decided to use them all because they were all so good.

The first comes from Benjamin Franklin:

"By failing to prepare, you are preparing to fail."[1]

This is so true. That's why it's crucial that we honestly look at ourselves, see our weak areas, and create a plan to overcome them. Without a plan, we can't help but fail. Planning is the first step to winning the fight.

Another great quote comes from John F. Kennedy:

"The time to repair the roof is when the sun is shining."[2]

You may not be facing a crisis today. However, the weak areas in your life could ultimately lead to difficult times. Why wait until you are broken to start making repairs? Today is the day to look at the weak areas in your life and start doing the work to fix them.

Finally, a quote from the Dallas Cowboys legendary coach Tom Landry (I can't believe I'm quoting a Dallas Cowboy):

"Setting a goal is not the main thing. It is deciding how you will go about achieving it and staying with that plan."[3]

That is my final challenge: create a prayerful plan for how you will become an unbreakable man of God and do all you can to stick to it.

Make that your New Year's Resolution.

SUNDAY
- [ ] Psalms 149-150

MONDAY
- [ ] Isaiah 63-64
- [ ] Mark 13

TUESDAY
- [ ] Isaiah 66-66
- [ ] Mark 14

WEDNESDAY
- [ ] Genesis 1-2
- [ ] Revelation 1

THURSDAY
- [ ] Genesis 3-4
- [ ] Revelation 2

FRIDAY
- [ ] Genesis 5-6
- [ ] Revelation 3

NOTES AND REFLECTION

MEMORY VERSE

Remember not the former things nor consider the things of old. Behold, I am doing a new thing; now it springs forth, do you not perceive it? I will make a way in the wilderness. and rivers in the desert. -Isaiah 43:18-19

Bibliography

Week 1

1. *"Top 70 Patrick Henry Quotes* (2024 Update)." Quote Fancy, quotefancy.com/patrick-henry-quotes
. Accessed 12 Aug. 2024.

Week 2

1. *Rocky III.* Directed by Sylvester Stallone, performances by Sylvester Stallone and Talia Shire, MGM/UA Entertainment Co., 1982.

Week 3

1. *Rocky III.* Directed by Sylvester Stallone, performances by Sylvester Stallone and Talia Shire, MGM/UA Entertainment Co., 1982.

Week 4

1. *"Courage, N. (1)." Merriam-Webster*, https://www.merriam-webster.com/dictionary/courage
. Accessed 12 July 2024.

Week 5

1. *"George Washington Quotes."* BrainyQuote.com. BrainyMedia Inc, 2024. 12 August 2024. https://www.brainyquote.com/quotes/george_washington_135801

Week 7

1. *"Best Martin Luther King Jr Quotes About Service to Others."* The Narratologist, www.thenarratologist.com/best-martin-luther-king-jr-quotes-about-service-to-others/. Accessed 13 Aug. 2024.

Week 8

1. *Creed III.* Directed by Michael B. Jordan, performances by Michael B. Jordan and Tessa Thompson, Metro-Goldwyn-Mayer, 2023.

Week 9

1. *Rocky IV.* Directed by Sylvester Stallone, performances by Sylvester Stallone and Talia Shire, MGM/UA Entertainment Co., 1985.

Week 10

1. *"Wild West Oasis." Vacation House Rules,* created by Scott McGillivray, season 5, episode 4, McGillivray Group, 2024.

Week 11

1. *Rocky Balboa.* Directed by Sylvester Stallone, performances by Sylvester Stallone and Burt Young, MGM Distribution Co. (United States) 20th Century Fox (International), 2006.

Week 13

1. *The Dark Knight Rises.* Christopher Nolan; Warner Bros., DC Entertainment; 2012. Film.

2. *Batman Begins.* Directed by Christopher Nolan, performances by Christian Bale and Michael Caine, Warner Bros. Pictures DC Comics Legendary Pictures Syncopy Patalex III Productions, 2005.

Week 14

1. *Bedtime Stories.* Directed by Adam Shankman, performances by Adam Sandler et al., Walt Disney Studios Motion Pictures, 2008.

2. Brewer, Jack. *"Issue Brief: Fatherlessness and It's Effects On American Society."* America First Policy, 15 May 2023, **https://americafirstpolicy.com/assets/uploads/ files/Issue_Breif_-_Fatherlessness_and_its_effects _on_American_society.pdf**

Week 16

1. *"Billy Graham Quotes."* BrainyQuote.com. BrainyMedia Inc, 2024. 12 August 2024. https://www.brainyquote.com/ quotes/billy_graham_150661

2. Witter, Brad. *"Rodney Dangerfield's 'I Don't Get No Respect' Was Inspired by His Rough Childhood."* Biography, 5 Feb. 2020, www.biography.com/actors/rodney-dangerfield-i-dont-get-no-respect. Accessed 11 Aug. 2024.

Week 17

1. *Creed II.* Directed by Steven Caple JR., performances by Michael B. Jordan and Sylvester Stallone, Metro-Goldwyn-Mayer New Line Cinema, 2018.

Week 18

1. *Creed II.* Directed by Steven Caple JR., performances by Michael B. Jordan and Sylvester Stallone, Metro-Goldwyn-Mayer New Line Cinema, 2018.

2. *"Newton's Third Law."* The Physics Classroom, **www.physicsclassroom.com/class/newtlaws/Lesson-4/ Newton-s-Third-Law**. Accessed 9 Aug. 2024.

Week 19

1. *"10 Times John Wayne Followed the Cowboy Code."* INSP, www.insp.com/blog/10-times-john-wayne-followed-the-cowboy-code/. Accessed 11 Aug. 2024.

Week 20

1. Schlereth, Mark, host. *"Just a Nice Healthy Quarterback Discussion" Stinkin' Truth Podcast,* Publisher, 08 July 2024, www.youtube.com/@stinkintruthpodcast

Week 22

1. *"Sell or Stay." Rehab Addict Rescue,* created by Nicole Curtis, season 1, episode 1, Bodega Productions, 2021.

Week 23

1. *Rocky IV.* Directed by Sylvester Stallone, performances by Sylvester Stallone and Talia Shire, MGM/UA Entertainment Co., 1985.

Week 24

1. *Creed.* Directed by Ryan Coogler, performances by Michael B. Jordan and Sylvester Stallone, Metro-Goldwyn-

Mayer Pictures New Line Cinema Chartoff-Winkler Productions, 2015.

Week 25

1. *Captain America: The First Avenger.* Directed by Joe Johnston, performances by Chris Evans and Tommy L. Jones, Paramount Pictures, 2011.

2. *Avengers: Endgame.* Directed by Anthony Russo and Joe Russo, performances by Robert L. Downey Jr and Chris Evans, Walt Disney Studios Motion Pictures, 2019.

3. *Donald C Stamps, Study Notes on Hebrews 12, Fire Bible: English Standard Version*, (Peabody, MA: Hendrickson Publishers Marketing, LLC, 2014), Pg 2160.

4. *"Blossom: Joey's "Whoa!" Catchphrase On 'Was From The TV Icon Gods' | PeopleTV."* Youtube, uploaded by Peopel, 11 Oct. 2017, youtu.be/wz66Cq_Hh-Q? si=nQ8getAvP-NaVuty.

Week 26

1. *"Thomas Jefferson Quotes."* BrainyQuote.com. BrainyMedia Inc, 2024. 13 August 2024. https://www.brainyquote.com/quotes/thomas_jefferson_141477.

Week 27

1. The Editors of the Encyclopedia Britannica. *"Text of the Declaration of Independence."* Britannica, 5 Jul. 2024, www.britannica.com/topic/Declaration-of-Independence/Text-of-the-Declaration-of-Independence. Accessed 12 Aug. 2024.

Week 28

1. *"Abraham Lincoln Quotes."* BrainyQuote.com. BrainyMedia Inc, 2024. 9 August 2024. https://www.brainyquote.com/quotes/abraham_lincoln_109275

Week 30

1. Swindoll, Charles R. *"Esther: A Woman of Strength and Dignity".* Thomas Nelson Publisher, 1997. p. 60.

Week 31

1. *Castaway.* Directed by Robert Zemeckis, performances by Tom Hanks and Helen Hunt, 20th Century Fox (North America) DreamWorks Pictures (International, through United International Pictures), 2000.

Week 33

1. *"John Quincy Adams Quotes."* BrainyQuote.com. BrainyMedia Inc, 2024. 11 August 2024. https://www.brainyquote.com/quotes/john_quincy_adams_122484.

Week 35

1. *"Mother Teresa Quotes About Success."* AZ Quotes, www.azquotes.com/author/14530-Mother_Teresa/tag/success. Accessed 12 Aug. 2024.

Week 36

1. *The Strive.* *"100+ MOTIVATIONAL JOCKO WILLINK QUOTES FOR GETTING AFTER IT."* The Strive, thestrive.co/best-jocko-willink-quotes/. Accessed 11 Aug. 2024.

Week 37

1. Yuan, Jada. *"Let's Roll."* New York Mag, 27 Jul. 2011, nymag.com/news/9-11/10th-anniversary/lets-roll/. Accessed 9 Aug. 2024.

2. "WEEKLY ADDRESS: Observing 9/11 with National Service." *The White House President Barack Obama*, 27 Jul. 2011, obamawhitehouse.archives.gov/the-press-office/2011/08/27/weekly-address-observing-911-national-service. Accessed 9 Aug. 2024.

Week 39

1. *Rocky III.* Directed by Sylvester Stallone, performances by Sylvester Stallone and Talia Shire, MGM/UA Entertainment Co., 1982.

Week 40

1. *Rocky Balboa.* Directed by Sylvester Stallone, performances by Sylvester Stallone and Burt Young, MGM Distribution Co. (United States) 20th Century Fox (International), 2006.

Week 41

1. *Apollo 13.* Directed by Ron Howard, performances by Tom Hanks et al., Universal Pictures, 1995.

Week 42

1. *"Whatcha Talkin Bout Willis."* Youtube, uploaded by Ukarau Kakepare, 16 Oct. 2007, youtu.be/Qw9oX-kZ_9k?si=-uwnrC1bjD5x5fBW.

Week 44

1. *Braveheart.* Directed by Mel Gibson , performances by Mel Gibson and Sophie Marceau, Paramount Pictures (United States and Canada) 20th Century Fox (International), 1995.

Week 45

1. *"Abraham Lincoln > Quotes > Quotable Quote."* Goodreads, **www.goodreads.com/quotes/43167-no-man-stands-so-tall-as-when-he-stoops-to**. Accessed 13 Aug. 2024.

Week 46

1. *Spider-Man: Homecoming.* Directed by John Watts, performances by Tom Holland and Michael Keaton, Columbia Pictures Marvel Studios Pascal Pictures, 2017.

2. *The Avengers.* Directed by Joss Whedon Whedon, performances by Robert Downey Jr., et al., Marvel Studios, 2012.

Week 47

1. *"Turkeys Away."* WKRP in Cincinnati, Created by Hugh Wilson, Season 1 Episode 7, MTM Enterprises, 1978.

Week 48

1. *Rocky V.* Directed by John G. Avildsen, performances by Sylvester Stallone and Talia Shire, MGM/UA Entertainment Co., 1990.

Week 49

1. *Rocky.* Directed by John G. Avildsen, performances by Sylvester Stallone and Talia Shire, United Artists, 1976.

Week 50

1. *"Noel." West Wing*, Created by Sorkin, Aaron, Season 2 Episode 10, John Wells Production, Warner Brothers Television, 2000.

Week 51

1. *Deck the Halls*. Directed by John Whitesell, performances by Danny DeVito and Matthew Broderick, 20th Century Fox, 2006.

Week 53

1. *"Benjamin Franklin Quotes."* BrainyQuote.com. BrainyMedia Inc, 2024. 13 August 2024. https://www.brainyquote.com/quotes/benjamin_franklin_138217.

2. *"John F. Kennedy Quotes."* BrainyQuote.com. BrainyMedia Inc, 2024. 13 August 2024. https://www.brainyquote.com/quotes/john_f_kennedy_110220.

3. *"Tom Landry Quotes."* BrainyQuote.com. BrainyMedia Inc, 2024. 13 August 2024. https://www.brainyquote.com/quotes/tom_landry_125246.

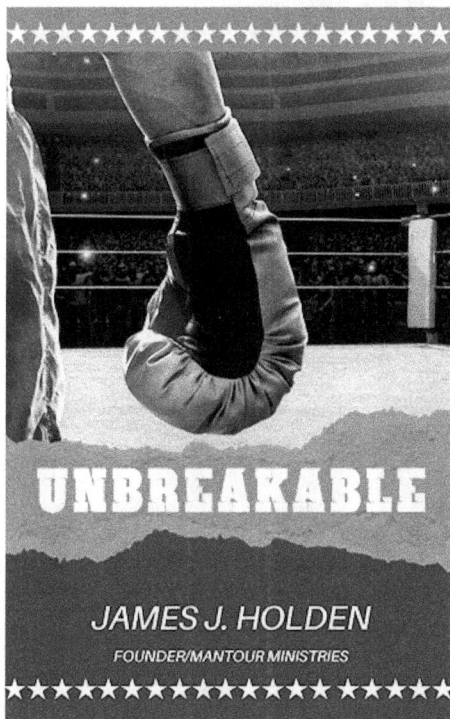

Also Available

UNBREAKABLE

JAMES J. HOLDEN

FOUNDER/MANTOUR MINISTRIES

IT'S TIME TO STAND FIRM AS

UNBREAKABLE MEN!

VISIT WWW.MANTOURMINISTRIES.COM/UNBREAKABLE

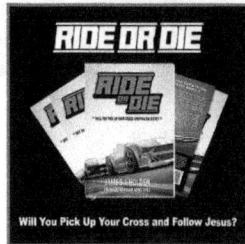

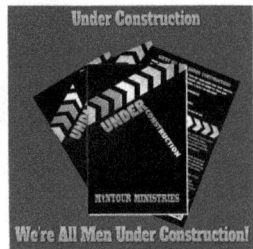

Jamie loves to speak to men and is available to speak at your next

men's event. Jamie combines humor and his personal testimony to engage and challenge men to grow in their walk with God. He uses his testimony of overcoming abuse and dealing with his physical and emotional issues growing up to encourage men that no matter what their background or where they have come from in life, they can grow into mighty men in God's kingdom.

"Years ago, while I was attending the University of Valley Forge, God gave me a deep desire to minister to men. My calling is to help men learn what it means to be a godly man and how to develop a deep, personal relationship with their heavenly Father. We strive to challenge and encourage men to reach their full potential in God's kingdom."

If you are interested in having Jamie at your next men's event as a speaker or workshop leader, or if you are interested in having him come share with your church, contact him by visiting www.mantourministries.com/invitejamie. He is also available to speak for one or multiple weeks on the theme of his books.

JOIN OUR MONTHLY FINANCIAL PARTNERS TEAM AND HELP US REACH EVEN MORE MEN!

JAMIE HOLDEN

FOUNDER/DIRECTOR, MANTOUR MINISTRIES

SCAN WITH PHONE CAMERA

GIVE ONLINE AT
HTTPS://WWW.MANTOURMINISTRIES.COM/PARTNER

www.ingramcontent.com/pod-product-compliance
Lightning Source LLC
Chambersburg PA
CBHW070032100426
42740CB00013B/2665